CRYOGENIC TREATMENT ON BRAKE ROTORS TO IMPROVE ITS WEAR RESISTANCE

Issue 19.07.2013

VIMLESH CHANDRAKANT AJBANI

CHAPTER 1

INTRODUCTION

Technological development have find out varieties of material but no one material satisfied enhanced service demand in all aspects and required further treatment to improve its various properties. It is very familiar with the heat treatment processes for to improve mechanical properties of material which require heating and subsequent cooling, now it will deal with an innovative technology of low temperature cooling and further heating and known as cryogenic treatment. The cryogenic treatment is modification of a material or component using cryogenic temperatures. Cryogenic processing makes changes to the crystal structure of materials. The major results of these changes are to enhance the abrasion resistance and fatigue resistance of the materials. This abrasion resistance increases wear resistance of brake rotor and its pad.

The cryogenic treatment of metals must certainly be regarded as one of the most important developments of the industrial age. It is one of the modern processes being used to treat metals as well as other materials. Until recently, cryogenic treatment was viewed as having little value, due to the often brittle nature of the finished product. It is only since the development of computer modeled cooling and reheating curves that the true benefits of cryogenically treated materials have realized by industry and the general public. Cryo treatment is a permanent, non-destructive, non- damaging process and not a coating which reduces abrasive wear, relieves internal stress, minimizes the susceptibility to micro cracking due to shock forces, lengthens part life, and increases performance. Cryo treated pieces are also less susceptible to corrosion. The cryogenic treatment process is a one-time, permanent treatment affecting the entire part, not just the surface.

1.1 HISTORY

Cryogenic processing has been around for many years but is truly in its infancy when compared to heat-treating. For centuries the Swiss would take advantage of the extremely low temperatures of the Alps to improve the behavior of their steels. They allow the steel to remain in the frigid regions of the Alps for long periods of time to improve its quality. Essentially, this was a crude aging process accelerated by the very low temperatures. What is understood to have happened was the reduction of the retained austenite and the increase in martensite. By performing this once secret process the Swiss obtained the reputation for producing a superior grade of steel.

Having said that, Swiss watchmakers and German machinists recognized from experience that metal properties were enhanced when allowed to "season" over a cold winter - sometimes packed in snow and placed in caves. The metals were stabilized and less prone to distortion when machined, enabling the critical tolerances in precision components (e.g. watch gears) to be held more closely. [1]

NASA engineers were the first to notice the effects of cold temperatures on materials. They noticed that many of the metal parts in the aircraft that had returned from the cold vacuum of space came back stronger than they were before flight. Since then sub-zero treatment (-80° C) has been used for many years, but with inconsistent results. Many of the inconsistencies were reduced by longer soaking periods and with deep cryogenic treatment (-190° C). [x] Cryogenic treatment has been around since the 1930"s, which was first documented when cryogenics was used on Jumo aircraft engine applications for Junkers airplanes, which were manufactured in Germany [2].

The concept of changing the properties of metals through the use of low temperature had its origins in this country back in World War II when the life of steel cutting tools was improved by immersing them in liquid nitrogen prior to being placed in service.[3] It was under the direction of Clarence Zener who would later go on to develop the Zener diode. At that time there were no computer controls so the steel tooling would be immersed in liquid nitrogen for a brief period of time, allowed to warm up, then placed into service. This method was crude and uncontrolled. Many of the tools would chip and break immediately upon use because the immersion process would create a very high thermal gradient in the tool and this would produce micro-cracks in the body. It was also later learned that the cryo-treatment would convert the retained austenite into un-tempered martensite. But the tools that would not break would experience a greatly enhanced service life. Today, the technique most commonly used involves gradual changes in temperature. Of course, anyone familiar with a Siberian winter might speculate that the Russians have been testing the theory of cryogenics for a very long time. Because the mechanisms involved have been poorly understood, more research is needed. Today, the technique most commonly used involves gradual changes in temperature rather than direct immersion. It is a fact that exposure to very low temperatures do produce permanent changes in materials. [4]

1.2 CLASSIFICATION OF TREATMENTS

TYPE A	TYPE B	TYPE C
Heat Treatment at High Temperature	Sub Zero or Cold Treatment at Low Temperature -80°C (193.15 K)	Deep Cryogenic Treatment at Low Temperature -193°C (80.15 K)
According to body treatment 1. Hardening 2. Tempering 3. Normalizing 4. Annealing	According to the methodology 1. Cryogen cooling by liquid nitrogen 2. Mechanical type Cascade refrigeration	According to the cryogen used 1. Nitrogen cooled 2. Hydrogen cooled
According to the surface treatment 1. Carburizing 2. Nitriding		According to the cryogenic system 1. Heat Exchanger 2. Direct Nebulization

1.3 ADVANTAGES OF CRYOGENIC TREATMENT [4] [I]

- Increased abrasive wear resistance
- Increased fatigue resistance
- Requires only one permanent treatment
- Changes the entire grain structure of the metal, not just the surfaces
- Refinishing or regrinds do not affect permanent improvements

- Eliminates thermal shock through a dry, computer controlled process
- Transforms most retained austenite to hard martensite
- Forms micro-fine carbide fillers to enhance carbide structures
- Increases durability and wear life
- Change in vibrational damping
- Increased electrical conductivity
- Stabilization and reduced warpage
- Decreases residual stresses in tool steels
- Decreases brittleness
- Increases tensile strength, toughness and stability
- Relaxes internal stresses
- Works on new or used tools
- Reduced down time, less maintenance and higher productivity
- Deep cryo processing is compatible with other treatments (TiN, Chrome, Teflon etc.)
- High alloy steel cutting tools stay sharper longer, fewer micro-cracks, less chipping
- Results in the orderly arrangement of crystals, increases internal bonding energy, and achieves a structural balance throughout the mass of the material

Cryo treating can make a major contribution to solving these problems:

1. High abrasive wear in cutting tools, moulds, dies, brake rotors, gears, engine components, etc.
2. High corrosive wear in chemical, food, and oil equipment applications.
3. High erosive wear from, water, slurries and other abrasive grit carriers.
4. Distortions induced by design, forming, machining or environment.
5. Stress relief in complex tools, components, and welds.
6. Stress relief cracking of weld zones.
7. Surface finishing in any application where long life is needed.
8. Stabilization in parts and components as a result of stresses.
9. Machinability in aluminium and copper parts.
10. Electrode life in copper resistance welding electrodes.

CHAPTER 2
LITERATURE REVIEW

2.1 THE CRYOGENIC TREATMENT CYCLE [5]

There is a persistent idea that cryogenic processing can be accomplished by immersing a part in liquid nitrogen. Research has shown that better results are obtained by a cycle where the temperature of the component being treated is slowly reduced. A generalized cycle of cryogenic processing is shown in Reference 2.1 the cycle has several steps including:

• Ramp down. In most cycles, the temperature is ramped down to 89K (-300°F, or -184°C) from ambient temperature in four to ten hours. This slow decent in temperature helps reduce the temperature gradient within the component and keeps stresses to a minimum. A slow descent to somewhere around –300F; this should take several hours. The reason for this is to make sure that the internal temperatures and surface temperatures of the object being treated do not differ significantly, thereby avoiding any possibility of cracking.

• Hold. The temperature is held at 89K for a period of time, typically from six to forty hours. It is well known that molecular activity is vastly reduced at very low temperatures. The long "soaking" time is believed to be necessary to allow both the fine carbides to precipitate, and the crystal lattice to achieve the lowest energy state possible. This is the point where the conversion from austenite to martensite occurs.

• Ramp up. The temperature is brought back to ambient over a period of four to ten hours. Then return to ambient temperature. Again, this can take from several hours to a day, for the same reasons expressed in step number one.

• Tempering. Tempering is used to temper any primary martensite that may have formed. Some materials require double or even triple tempering. The tempering cycle is not always required. Tempering temperatures and times vary with the material and the size of the part being tempered. Tempering occurs at an elevated temperature. Since we now have new primary martensite from the completed conversion process, this material needs to be tempered to avoid brittleness, just as with a conventional heat treatment. Specific elevated temperatures are based on the material being conditioned.

2.2 METALLURGICAL CHANGE [6]

To understand the effects of cryogenic processing it is essential that one be acquainted with the heat treating of metals. The primary reason for heat treating steel is to improve its wear resistance through hardening. Gears, bearings, and tooling for example are hardened because they need excellent wear resistance for extended reliability and performance. The steps in heat-treating are frequently explained in a simplistic manner but it takes significant skill and experience to execute heat treatments successfully.

Steel will normally be raised in temperature to the austenizing temperature, usually 1600°F or higher. Austenite is a soft phase of steel and malleable – hence it is very easy to wear the structure down with repeated use, therefore the need for heat-treating. Gears and other tooling are often rough machined or formed in the austenitic state. After a predetermined period of time at elevated temperature, that is determined by the phase diagram of the alloy in question, the material will be quenched in a bath that may be oil, water, brine or polymeric compounds. The rapid cooling (quenching) of the steel in the quenching medium will cause the atoms in the microstructure to rearrange in the atomic structure that is called martensite. Reference 2.3 shows a representation of the atomic structure of both the austenitic and martensitic phase. A close analogy to this is coal and diamond. They are both made up of primarily carbon atoms. In coal the carbon atoms are in a very loose arrangement and have very few cross-links to one another, this makes them readily available to be taken away by wear or some other reaction like heat. In a diamond the carbon atoms have a very different bonding arrangement making it the hardest substance known.

The studies have shown that cryogenic treatment produces metallurgical changes in the microstructure of steel. These changes are the principal reasons for the dramatic improvement in wear resistance. As greater amounts of retained austenite are transformed, and the amount of martensite is increased, the material obtains a more uniform hardness. The studies have shown that hardness is not increased appreciably in the material being treated but the consistency of the hardness is greatly improved. The surface energy of martensite is higher than that of austenite due to the differences in their atomic structures. Austenite has a Face-Centered-Cubic crystalline structure and martensite has a Body-Centered-Tetragonal crystalline structure. In adhesive wear situations, the martensite is less likely to „tear" out than is austenite. The probability of wear particles forming in steel in which the austenite has been transformed to martensite is less than for steel containing some retained austenite.

A second effect is the precipitation of fine eta (η) carbide particles. Research (6) has shown that these fine eta carbide particles are precipitated during the long cryogenic soak. These are in addition to the larger carbide particles present before cryogenic treatment. These fine particles or "fillers", along with the larger particles, form a denser, more coherent and tougher matrix in the material. The adhesive wear coefficient is decreased, and the wear rate is decreased as measured by standard pin- on-disk wear tests. In abrasive wear situations, both the martensite formation and the fine carbide formation work together to reduce wear. The additional fine carbide particles particles help support the martensite matrix, making it more difficult to abrade lumps of material. When a foreign particle is squeezed onto the surface, the carbide matrix resists plowing, thereby reducing wear.

2.3 EFFECTS ON THE MECHANICAL PROPERTIES [7]

An extensive collection of CT test results in concerning hardness and wear resistance of a wide range of steel grades. This paper represents a milestone in the CT field. The papers show wear and hardness results for respectively twelve tool steels, three stainless steels and four other steels. By comparing the results obtained with 189 K SCT and 77 K DCT, the authors have observed a significant abrasive resistance increase for the tool steels subjected to the colder treatment.

2.3.1 WEAR RESISTANCE

Wear resistance represents an important property of a material when it is used in applications that lead to reciprocal moving of in-contact components, such as machining tools, bearings, gears, brake rotors, piston seals, etc. Among the listed above microstructural changes related to CT, both retained austenite reduction and carbide precipitation can lead to an improvement in wear resistance by the increase of the steel hardness. It is almost impossible to carry out a complete comparison between the results obtained in literature, because of different test conditions such as sliding velocity, distance or applied load used by the authors and different wear indicators reported reported as results i.e. wear rate or wear resistance. The most experimented effect of CT is the enhancement of the wear resistance, especially on tool steels. Table 2.2 shows the wear resistance improvement reported in literature, after the publications about different materials and test for reference duration. Different setup are reported in literature for wear test, but the most used for reference duration is the pin on disk, according to the ASTM standards and the results are usually reported in terms of wear resistance or of wear rate. Some authors have also performed tests directly on cryo-treated tools, by measuring the tool life in number of worked pieces, in the so-called "flank-wear test" or in the "twist drill test". As it is shown in Table 2.2 one of the most cryo-tested materials is AISI M2 high speed tool steel, which is widely used for drills, milling cutters and other tools. Wear resistance is an important property not only for tools, but also for many components subjected to rolling or sliding contact, in different industrial fields like automotive, mining, oil drilling, etc. Some studies about effects of CT on bearing steels and carburized steels used in automotive industries are available in literature (i.e. En353 has a significant application for crown wheel, crown pinion, bevel pinion, bevel wheel, timing gears, king pinion, pinion shaft). Many authors agree with about the reason of the wear resistance improvement: it is the fine carbides precipitation that enhances strength and toughness of the martensite matrix, rather than the reduction or the elimination of the retained austenite fraction.

Another interesting comparison has been proposed in between cryo-treated and TiN coated samples, which have shown that CT for 24 hours at 93 K is more effective on wear resistance than TiN coating. Through the comparison of the results of CT specimens treated with different parameters, the authors have also concluded that the mechanism responsible for the wear resistance improvement is essentially an isothermal process and the soaking time is more important than the minimum temperature reached during the treatment. In addition, they have found CT to be more beneficial on untempered than on tempered samples. The influence of the soaking temperature on DCT wear improvement has been confirmed in. The wear resistance of some engineering polymers and composites can be improved by DCT. The authors have obtained an increase up to 60% in abrasive wear resistance of cryo-treated PTFE, while PEI and PI have shown improvements up to 35% and 58% respectively. In particular, the paper focus on the different responses to DCT, which have been obtained for the same polymeric matrix combined with different amounts and qualities of fibers or qualities of fibers or fillers. As an example, a +30% in wear resistance have been reported for cryo-treated PEI without fiber reinforcement, while the same material 40% glass fibers reinforced have shown a –35% in wear performance after DCT. Some interesting results have been reported, in the same paper, for Polyetherimide Copolymer, for Polyurethane (PU) and for Polycarbonate.

2.3.2 HARDNESS

Many hardness tests about CT are reported in literature because this property is related to the wear resistance. Hardness properties are usually measured through indentation tests and they are expressed in different scales depending on the penetrator shape. The most used methods are the Rockwell and the Vickers ones. While the first method is a macro indentation test, the second one can be performed both as macro or micro-indentation, depending on the applied load, as performed. The hardness of a tool steel is mainly influenced by retained austenite and in this way CT can play an important role. However, when compared to wear results, hardness test results, indicate that the mechanisms can be different for different materials.

For instance, in a little increase (+0.13%) in hardness has induced a –51% in wear rate for AISI M2 and the authors have concluded that AISI M2 wear resistance improvement can be attributed to hardness increase. The same test on AISI H13 tool steel has shown an improvement of 6.9% in hardness related to a decrease of 29% in wear rate and, according to the authors, the wear resistance improvement has been correlated to the enhanced toughness of the CT material. [1] The paper suggests that playing on carbides fraction and dimension and on retained austenite allows achieving an optimized ratio between hardness and toughness in high speed steels. Interesting results on HSS base composites reinforced with Nb and Ta carbides have been obtained, with about 10% increased hardness. Concerning non-ferrous materials, no significant changes in hardness of aluminum alloys and of Ultra-high Molecular Weight Polyethylene have been detected, while PTFE, PEI, PI, PU and PC have shown important changes in hardness.

2.3.3 TENSILE AND BENDING STRENGTH

A few tensile and bending test results have been published comparing properties before and after CT. This is mainly due to the fact that tensile properties are less relevant than hardness and wear resistance in tool steels, which are the most studied materials in the CT literature. Furthermore, static properties are expected to be not strongly affected by retained austenite fraction, while concerning precipitation strengthening it is supposed that very small precipitates can be easily bypassed at high stress levels by the dislocation climbing mechanism. However, the only published results about tool steel refer to AISI M2 and T1 and indicate a remarkable improvement of about 20% and of 25% respectively in bending strength. In, an increase from 7% to 16% in tensile strength of 4140 cold rolled steel specimens has been detected after CT. A slight reduction in tensile strength has been measured for a carburized steel-815M17 subjected to CT, compared to the same material conventionally treated. In particular the authors have observed a decrease of 1.5% for SCT and of 9.34% for DCT. The cryogenic treatment does not seem to be effective on tensile properties of AISI 304 and 316 stainless steels. No significant changes in tensile properties have been detected on aluminum alloys and on UHMWPE.

2.3.4 FATIGUE RESISTANCE

Fatigue of materials has been one of the most important research topics from the beginning of the 20th century until today in the area of materials and mechanical engineering. All the above listed CT microstructural changes are related to the fatigue behavior, someone with beneficial effects and other ones with detrimental effects. A field of fine hard carbides or the presence of nano-sized martensite in an austenitic matrix can be the effective mechanisms in delaying or blocking dislocations motion at low stress amplitude, when dislocation climbing is unlikely to appear. From this point of view, on the one hand the observed DCT fine carbides precipitation can lead to a prolonged crack nucleation phase. On the other hand, the retained fraction of ductile austenite can act as a crack arrestor in the propagation phase and then its reduction could have a detrimental effect on the final stage of fatigue. In addition, the residual stresses too play an important role in crack nucleation mechanism, in particular during the bending fatigue. Therefore it is necessary to weigh up all these effects, in order to understand the fatigue results. Despite of their great importance in many mechanical applications, fatigue properties of CT steels have not been investigated by many authors is the oldest paper found in literature about low temperature treatment and fatigue fatigue strength. The authors have subjected cold rolled steel to two different DCT: a rapid treatment by direct immersion in liquid nitrogen for 1 hour, a slow treatment by controlled cooling and 30 minutes holding time. Bending fatigue test results on treated and non-treated specimens have shown no differences in mean values of fatigue limit, but a smaller dispersion for DCT samples has been found. In addition, the authors have carried out an acoustic spectra analysis finding clear differences in the amplitude of harmonics of DCT specimens, but no microstructural changes have been detected in metallographic and fractographic inspections. For this reason the authors have suggested a residual stresses effect, supposing a connection with the redistribution of the lattice defects. Some studies about CT and fatigue have been conducted at the Precision and Intelligence Laboratory of the Tokyo Institute of Technology. During these researches the authors have measured the Ms (martensite start temperature) of a stainless steel with the acoustic emission technique, then they have cooled the samples just 3 K above Ms and they have returned the samples to the room temperature. In the test has been conducted on an austenitic Fe-18Cr-8Ni stainless steel pre-strained by 2% in order to increase the dislocation density. The result, as reported in have shown that the CT does not increase the fatigue life in the low-cycle regime (< 10^4 cycles). However, CT samples have shown longer life in high-cycle regime (> 10^4 cycles). Considering a maximum stress of 350 MPa, the number of cycles to failure is about four and five times larger in CT specimens than in non-treated ones. In addition, the authors have found that at a maximum stress of 310 MPa (just above the fatigue limit), the number of cycles to failure has been $2.8*10^5$ for non-treated samples whereas subzero treated specimen did not fail at $1.7*10^7$ cycles, (> 60 times longer). In, the same material has been pre-strained by 10% and subjected to the same subzero treatment, obtaining an extension of fatigue life of more than 10 times. Similar results have been found on AISI 304 (2% and 10% pre- strained) and on AISI 316 samples. The authors have stated that by controlling dislocation density and temperature it is possible to control the size of martensite in the material; they have also suggested that the nano-sized martensite formed at intersection of two partial dislocations is effective in pinning dislocation, with the result of extending fatigue life by prolonging the nucleation phase. A slight increase (25-30 MPa on about 600 MPa) in fatigue limit has been also measured in for the rotating fatigue test on AISI 4340 steel. The authors have attributed this result to the slight increase in hardness, but they did not propose any microstructural and mechanism for the explanation of the phenomenon. Concerning non-ferrous materials, a high- cycle fatigue test has been performed at room temperature on an unspecified aluminum alloy as-welded and cryo-treated, which has not shown a noticeable improvement.

2.3.5 THERMAL FATIGUE RESISTANCE

In many engineering applications, in particular for internal combustion engines, the combination of thermal and mechanical cycles is a normal operational requirement and therefore it could be interesting to perform an analysis of CT effects on the thermo mechanical fatigue behavior of materials. Nevertheless, the only study which has been published until now is a preliminary test about effect of DCT on pure thermal fatigue properties, without mechanical loads. By subjecting a rotating disk to a cyclic induction-warming and water-cooling (from 353 K to 973 K) a crack network has been generated on its surface. After measuring the thermal crack density, the mean crack length and the maximum crack length, the authors have calculated the pyrocracking factor *C* as the product of these values. The DCT disk has shown a pyrocracking factor of 0.6 μm against 1.18 μm of the untreated one. The parameter responsible for this decrease has been the crack density, which has reduced from 3.49 mm^{-1} to 1.53 $mm.^{-1}$ .The mean crack length and the maximum crack length have remained almost the same for DCT and non-DCT samples, leading the authors to conclude that DCT can delay the crack nucleation process without increasing the propagation.

2.3.6 FRACTURE TOUGHNESS

Fracture toughness is a measure of the breaking resistance of a material which contains a crack. Together with the fatigue behavior, fracture toughness is one of the keys of the design applications of the last century. As mentioned in the Fatigue Resistance paragraph, retained ductile austenite fraction can play the role of crack arrestor in martensitic steels, enhancing the toughness. The authors have suggested that carbides fraction and dimension and retained austenite fraction play an important role in the optimization of the ratio between hardness and toughness of high speed materials steels. The authors did not perform any test to measure fracture toughness *KIC*, but they have used a semi-empirical equation proposed by themselves to calculate it, pointing out a decrease in toughness after CT.

Where *HRc* is the Rockwell-C hardness, *fcarb* and *faust* the volume fractions of undissolved eutectic carbides and retained austenite, *E* the Young elastic modulus expressed in MPa, and *dp* is the mean distance between undissolved eutectic carbides in the matrix. The value of *dp* has been estimated by the authors by measuring the mean diameter of undissolved carbides *Dp* from a 1000x magnification image obtained with a Scanning Electron Microscope (SEM).

It is evident that a higher fraction of smaller carbides leads to lower values of *dp* and *KIC*. It is also evident the role played by *dp*, *fcarb* and *faust* in controlling the ratio between *HRc* and *KIC*. In contrast with the results of, the Charpy impact tests reported in have shown an increase of *KIC* on AISI H13 tool steel after a double tempering and a DCT, without any effect on hardness and impact energy. The impact toughness before and after DCT on M2 and T1 tool steels has been measured in , obtaining an increase of about 43% and 58% respectively. No DCT effect on toughness has been found on 4140 cold rolled steel. An evident toughness drop (14.3%) after DCT has been observed in on AISI 4340 steel; the authors have attributed this decrease to the higher martensite content of the cryo-treated samples. A slight increase (+11.8%) of the impact toughness *J* after 48 hours DCT on a 7075 aluminum alloy has been measured in, with a confidence level of about 90-95%.

2.4 APPLICATIONS OF CRYOGENIC TREATMENT [II]

Cryogenic processing can benefit virtually every industry, and new applications are being discovered every day. Here are just a few:

Motorsports-Automotive and Engine Components

Transmission assemblies, Planetary gears, Ring, Wheel bearings, Ball bearings, Hub assemblies, Brake rotors, Brake pads, Drive shafts, Axles, Tires, U-joints, Yoke, Clutch plates, Clutch pressure plates. Specific to engines, Engine Blocks, Connecting rods, Wrist pins, Pistons, Rings, Crankshafts, Camshafts, Push rods, Rocker arms, Roller bearings, Valves, Valve springs, Cylinder sleeves, Spark Plugs, Copper spark plug wires, Radiators, Turbochargers, Exhaust manifolds, Cylinder heads and Intake manifolds.

Marine

Propellers, Transmissions, Lower drive units, Impellers, Shafts, Inboard and Outboard jet pumps

Industry Machining and Tooling Cutting Tools

Band saw blades, Broaches, Castings, Chain saw blades, Chipper knives, Cutting dies, Drills, Die castings, End mills, Forgings, Gear cutters, Guillotine knives, Hobs, Knives, Piercing tools, Planer blades, Punches, Reamers, Router bits, Saw blades, Slitter knives, Slotting cutters, Stamping tools, Steel rule die, Taps, Thread chasers.

Carbide Inserts and Cutting Tools

Carbide Chipper knives, Carbide cutting dies, Carbide drills, Carbide blanking dies, Carbide end mills, Carbide inserts, Carbide piercing tools, Carbide punches, carbide, reamers, Carbide router bits, Carbide stamping dies, Carbide stamping tools, Carbide tipped saw blades.

Punch Press Tools - Brake Press - Shears

Blanking dies, Brake dies, Cut off knives, Die springs, Dies, Die casting dies, Draw dies, Form tools, Insert tools, Punches, Roll form tools, Shear blades, Stamping dies, Turret press tools.

Welding & Contacts

Wire feed nozzles and tips, Wire guides, Wire tubes, plasma cutting tips and nozzles, electrodes, Laser cutting nozzles, Water jet nozzles and Sand blasting nozzles.

Plastics and Plastics Industry

Bias cutters, Circular blades, Core pins, Cutting dies, Dicers, Ejector pins, Extrusion equipment, Granulator blades, Granulator screens, Injection moulds, Milling cutters, Nylon panty hose, Pulverizing knives, Router bits, Shredder knives, Shredder screens,

Slitter blades, Teflon, Weed wicker trimmer line, Trimmers.

Paper Industry

Arbours, Chipper knives, Circular perforating wheels, Cut off knives, Envelope dies, Guillotine knives, Jordan bars, Label dies, Paper drills, Perforators, Punches, Razor blades, Saw Blades, Shifters, Shredder blades, Slitter knives, Slitter knives, Steel rule dies, Tape cutters, Tissue perforators, Trimmers, Valves.

Woodworking

Band saw blades, Chain saw blades, chipper knives, Chisels, Circular saw blades, Dado blades, Files, Forming blades, Forster bits, Jig saw blades, Moulding cutters, Reciprocating blades, Saw blades, Sewall blades, Scroll saw blades, Shaping cutters, Planes.

Nonferrous Metals

Aluminium, Brass, Bronze, Carbide, Cobalt, Titanium.

Textiles

Arbours, Bearings, Bobbins, Conveyors, Cut off knives, Grippers, Guillotine knives, Label dies, Needles, Perforating wheels, Punches, Razor blades, Slitter knives, Steel rule, Dies, Tape cutters, Trimmers.

Stress Relief

Aluminium, Brass, Casting, Copper, Dies, Forgings, Machine parts, Iron, Mouldings, Plastics, Precision ground parts, Steel, Welded parts.

Firearms – Weapons

This category includes Knives, Firearms, Aluminium arrow shafts, Arrow points, Firing mechanisms, Pistol barrels, Revolver barrels, Rifle barrels, Shotgun barrels, Bullets, Dies, Actions.

Sports Equipment

This category includes Baseball bats, Softball bats, Golf clubs, Golf balls, Roller blade wheels, Skate blades, urethane wheels, Bearings, Bicycle components, Tennis rackets, RC electric motors, Nylon string, Fishing line, Fishing hooks.

Musical Instruments

Brass horns, mouthpieces, strings, bells, cymbals, lead pipes and more.

Agriculture

Blades, Mower blades, Chain saw blades, Concrete saw, Concrete saw teeth, asphalt grinding teeth, Bucket teeth, Cultivator points, Forks, Harrow blades, Plough points, Ploughshares, Roller chain, Spades and Tines.

Aerospace - Aeronautics

Castings and Components, Engines, Landing gear, Supports, Propellers, Turbine blades, Hydraulic pumps, Bearings, Turbochargers.

Electronics - Audio

Stereo speakers, Transformers, Cabling and Cords, Electronic components, Printed circuit boards, Vacuum tubes, Amplifiers, Receivers, Pre-amps, Tuners, Crossovers,

Power supplies, CD players, CD's, DVD players, Power cords, Interconnect cables, Speaker cables, Isolation tables, Switches, Contacts, Flexible Circuits, AC receptacles, Copper wire, Power strips.

2.4.1 GEARS [6]

A study by the IIT Research Institute published in November 1995 for the Instrumented Factory for Gears sponsored by the US Army ManTech was conducted to „study the effects of the carburizing process and cryogenics treatments in modifying the microstructure of the material". The results of the tests as presented at the INFAC Industry briefing, June 13, 2000 were that the deep cryogenic treatment gave 50% extra pitting resistance, 5% more load carrying capacity, and a 40°F to 60°F higher tempering temperature. Although these experiments were performed on AISI 9310 material (standard helicopter transmission gear material) the conclusions show promising results which may be applicable to the general subject of mechanical and chemical wear resistance.

2.4.2 BEARINGS [6]

An article published in Lubrication Engineering October 2002, investigates the effects of strain hardening and retained austenite transformation, both of which are triggered by rolling contact, on the fatigue life of 52100 bearing steel. The conclusion of the paper was that the origin of residual stress generated due to rolling contact is associated with phase transformation. The past assumptions were that strain hardening was the primary cause of the generation of residual stress. The fact that the amount of retained austenite correlates with the life of the bearing is one of the factors taken into consideration. The tie in here from a multitude of other research is that cryogenic processing converts retained austenite into martensite. Therefore, cryogenic processing eliminates the primary mechanism for the generation of residual stresses in ball bearings due to rolling contact. Of course, the majority of bearings never even reach their L10 life, because of factors such as contamination, improper lubrication, and incorrect installation. However, once we solve some of those man-made "bearing- killers", perhaps cryo-treating will present the next opportunity to extend life even further, beyond the typical expectations.

2.4.3 BRAKE ROTOR [9]

In this paper reported benefits are impressive, a good example being cast iron disc brake rotors. Diversified Cryogenics in the US conducted a back -to- back test of brake otherwise identical 13-inch brake discs, one of which had been cryogenically tempered and the other not. The untreated disc was run over 50 laps of Brainerd International Raceway using a racing friction material, at the completion of which the disc was sufficiently badly scored and cracked to be deemed unsafe, it was scrap. The treated disc was run for 56 laps with the same friction material and then an additional 35 laps with street pads, 91 laps in total, at the completion of which it was judged good for a further 40 laps. In other words, the working life of the disc had been increased by a factor of 2.6. Because of the reduced warping and cracking of the disc, pad wear was also reduced by 40%. Similar improvements have been reported from racing users, a doubling of disc and pad life being typical. In street use the improvements can be even greater. Cryocon Inc in the US has reported ambulance, taxi, police and other fleet operators enjoying increases in brake rotor service life of three to four times. Greg Bartlett of Frozen Solid sounds a warning, though, about the results being inconsistent from one disc manufacturer to another. Presumably because of differences in the constitution of the cast iron (certain trace elements such as titanium is known to have a significant influence on rotor performance), some manufacturers" discs show more pronounced improvements than others.

2.4.4 PLASTICS [II]

Cryogenically treated plastics have several desirable attributes. First, plastics themselves will become stronger and more durable. What happens when a plastic part is made, during the solidification stage, some of the molecules get caught in a random pattern. But molecules move at subzero and deep cryogenic temperatures, albeit slowly. Liken it if you will to water freezing or crystallizing as it turns to ice. The material molecules do move and form into a tighter denser, realigned pattern. When returned to room temperature, the molecules stay in the new relationship, producing less random and more even spacing which in turn reduces the open areas between the grid matrixes to one another. The resulting product possesses a better wear pattern and an improved bonding of molecules to each another. And this is a one-time process that treats the part all the way through. It is not just a surface treatment. Another effect is the smoothing action on the surface of the material being processed. During the realignment, the molecules at the surface also close ranks, resulting in a structural change in the surface. The peaks and valleys don't disappear but they do flatten out considerably. This causes less friction, and less wear. Panty hose are on the list because they get tougher and becomes less more resistant to runs.

Testing on all of the various plastic grades is not yet conclusive. Nylon and Teflon work well, but the multitude of other grades need to be tested and proven. Teflon for a torch tip is being tested and shows promise.

2.4.5 TOOL STEEL [13]

The materials like one high speed steel (M1) used for lathe tools, milling cutters, cutter blades, boring tools, twist drills, metal cutting saws etc; one constructional steel (EN19) used for axle shafts, gears, connecting rods, studs, bolts and propeller shaft joint etc and one chromium hot work steel (H13) used for making cutters; were selected to study the improvements in wear resistance. The samples were treated at 0° C, -20° C, - 40° C, -80° C and -190° C. The wear resistance improvement varied from in total material are 315% to 382% depending upon the material tested. Therefore, further investigations can be continued with any other material to investigate the improvements in wear resistance by cryogenic treatment.

Samples of 50 mm length were made from standard bar stock of 8 - 12 mm diameter procured locally. The samples were heat treated separately as per prescribed ASM standards. The samples were divided into six sets. The first set of samples after treatment and tempering were kept as reference for measuring the improvements in wear resistance at different temperature treatments. The second set of the samples were cooled down to 0°C slowly at a rate of 0.9 K/min, the third to - 20°C, the fourth to -40°C, the fifth to -80°C and the sixth to -190°C. All the samples were soaked at the respective temperatures for 24 h and slowly brought back to room temperature and retempered.

The wear test apparatus is shown in schematically in Reference 2.9, while the weights and other components are shown in Reference 2.8. Each sample was abraded for 3 min against a course grinding wheel of outer diameter 50mm, running at 200 rpm under a load of 20N. Each sample was weighed before and after every abrasion period, using analytical balance with accuracy up to two digits. The analyses are presented in Tables, the results are summarised in Reference 2.11.

2.4.6 WELDING ELECTRODES & CONTACTS [II]

Cryogenic treatment greatly improves the wear resistance and life expectancy of copper alloy resistance welding electrodes. Resistance to deformation is also greatly enhanced, and less input power is required to operate the weld operation. Another great benefit is that tip burn-off is greatly reduced.

The typical mode of failure for welding electrodes is thermal cyclic fatigue. The part is heated and cooled many times which causes cracks to form. The cracks then propagate and the surface starts to collapse. This changes the surface area which throws off the welding parameters and the part starts to fail rapidly. Cryogenic processing delays the initial cracking and reduces the resistivity of the part. The increased life reduces welding costs and increases profits. It also improves the quality of the weld.

Documented test cases show at least a 100% life expectancy increase for copper alloy electrodes, but many users report a 300% life increase.

There are several other areas in the welding field to consider. First and the most obvious are weldments themselves. Cryogenic Processing removes weld stress and deadens the pulling and tugging that accompany the welding process.

Other areas for welders are the wire guides, wire tubes, and nozzles on wire feed welding machines. The nozzles wear longer and better. Plasma cutting equipment tips and nozzles are great candidates for increased wear. Laser cutting nozzles and water jet nozzles are being studied, but proven results have already been seen in sand blasting nozzles, pressure washer nozzles, and paint and powder coating nozzles last longer once processed.

2.4.7 MUSIC WIRE

Cryogenic Treatment is a very low temperature treatment applied to metallic alloys to improve its mechanical properties through phase change, stress relief and the formation of micro-precipitates. Although this treatment process has been gaining popularity in the last two decades, this technique has been largely confined to steels and ferrous metals. However, recent work has shown the treatment to have an effect on other materials such as copper, tungsten-carbide, and even polymers like Teflon. This has led to the process being applied to an array of materials and applications, including cutting tools, welding electrodes and race car engine parts. Recently there have been attempts amongst musical instrument makers, musicians and cryogenic treatment service providers to perform cryogenic treatment on musical instruments. While there are claims that these instruments experienced improved tonal performance after Cryogenic treatment, there have been no attempts to examine and quantify these claims. This study is an effort to characterize music wire (guitar strings) before and after cryogenic treatment. Improvements due to the treatment process are evaluated according to changes in acoustic, mechanical and material properties. Also, in the process, a novel approach to the acoustic analysis of music wire was developed.

2.4.8 ENGINE [II]

Treated engine components will have increases wear resistance, but the real gain is in relief of residual stresses. Every part and component undergoes extreme machining, forging, casting, and forming during manufacturing, all of which induce residual stress into the component. During operation, an engine undergoes immense heat and pressures every time the spark plug fires, the fuel ignites and combustion occurs. The heat build-up and dimensional forces are the causes of friction, wear, and uneven power utilization which are the primary factors in overall engine performance and life expectancy. Cryogenics can help overcome these manufacturing "flows" and internal stresses imposed on the engine by tightening grain structure, reducing internal vibration, transferring energy more efficiently and dissipating heat faster. This allows the engine to run smoother, cooler, more efficiently and best of all helps reduce engine failure. The results are dramatic! The engine gained a 5% increase in power with a peak increase of 13 horsepower after cryogenic treatment. The most noticeable gain was at 7900 RPM with a net gain of 18.1 horsepower.

2.4.9 SPRING [4]

Not unexpectedly, chassis springs are also affected by cryogenic processing. Chassis springs lose their spring constant during a race. This can cause the chassis to lose its cornering ability, which drastically slows the car. Loss of spring constant also alters the height or road clearance of the vehicle. The vehicle height is critical at high speeds because it has a big affect on the aerodynamics of the car, and hence on the handling and the top speed of the car.

Further advantage for cryogenic processing of springs is that the process seems to eliminate or reduce harmonic vibrations. If you have ever seen a high-speed movie of a valve spring at high engine rpm, you will notice that the springs do not simply move up and down. It does a very complex hula dance because of the harmonic vibrations. Racers typically have to design the spring and valve trains so that harmonics do not interfere with the valve action. Springs do not simply move up and down. It does a very complex hula dance because of the harmonic vibrations. Racers typically have to design the spring and valve trains so that harmonics do not interfere with the valve action.

2.4.10 ELECTRONICS - AUDIO COMPONENTS [II]

Cryogenics changes the way current flows in a conductor. Aluminium, brass, copper, tin, and lead used in the electronics industry are affected by cryogenics. All of these materials exhibit longer wear, and more durability, but they also exhibit a better conductivity rating. When these materials are in the molten state during the metal-making process, as the solidification takes place, some molecules get caught in a random pattern. And we know that molecules do move about at sub- zero and deep cryogenic temperatures, albeit slowly. Like it if you will to water freezing or crystallizing as it turns to ice. The molecules move to form into a tighter, realigned pattern. Upon returning to room temperature, the molecules stay in this new relationship, producing less random, more even spacing, which in turn reduces the open areas between the grid matrixes to one another. The resulting product exhibits a better electrical current flow. It also strengthens solder to make their joints stronger and less subject to lifting. The printed circuit board material itself loses the stress it has which helps the board last longer and puts less strain on component parts. The increase in conductivity has been measured between 5% and 10%. This helps cabling, wire, solder runs, and transformers to operate more efficiently.

Cryogenic treatment of stereo components produces a permanent change to the component that allows your system to transmit much more information. The result is improved sound reproduction without sacrificing any sound quality you presently enjoy, better imaging and staging, greater separation of individual voices, richer colouring, more presence and impact, greater clarity without loss of warmth, more definition in the upper and lower registers without added shrillness or booziness.

For stereo speakers, the same stress that limits a trumpet from resonating properly is removed to allow the speaker to vibrate evenly. The proper combination is to treat the speaker and the metal support structure as a unit to allow the stresses to release in both parts, taking the tugs and pulls out of the system. Music from CDs is richer and deeper in tonal attributes. Transformer magnetic cores saturate to a lesser extent, and there is a lower hysteresis in transformers.

Tests by major companies found advantages. Tests done by Boeing, Sunstrand demonstrated cryogenic processing extended the life of circuit boards in military applications, specifically boards used in cruise missiles. Tests done by Honeywell on experimental thin film magnetic memory wafers showed increased conductivity of metallic layers, reduced residual stress between layers, and possible "healing" of vacancies in the layers. Tests on transformers showed treated transformers had significantly less hysteresis. The magnetic core saturated less. Tests on transistors showed a decrease in rise time. Other tests indicate greatly increased contact life on relays, switches, and circuit breakers. Parts with plastic fascias should have the fascia loosened to prevent breakage due to differential contraction between the plastic and the metal chassis. Audio components will require a break-in period before optimum sound is achieved and may extend longer than the manufacturer suggests. All items that have previous break-in must have a second break-in period.

2.4.11 STRESS RELIEF [III]

Residual stresses exist in all metals and metal components. Cryogenic treatment relieves these stresses. This is found in observations made by Einstein and Bose of Germany. Both of these noted physicists observed that matter is at its most relaxed state or condition when it has the least amount of kinetic energy. [10] The process of freezing is not one of putting cold into an object. Rather, it is the removal of heat. When one remove heat, removing energy and slowing down the molecular activity i.e. kinetic energy of the object being frozen. This is evident to every high school science student who studies the effects of heat and its removal on water.

Absolute zero, which is –459 ° F or 0 ° Kelvin, is that point where no further energy can be extracted. Many people believe that at absolute zero there is no kinetic energy at all. This is not the case. But absolute zero provides a theoretical point where matter is at its most relaxed state.

Cryogenic treatment with liquid nitrogen does not get the material to its absolute lowest temperature, but when we bring materials to –300° F to –320° F for extended periods, we have removed a large amount of the objects latent heat, slowed down its kinetic energy, and relieved or relaxed many of the residual stresses that exist within it. At this point, cryogenic treatment has relieved residual stresses. There are a large number of cryogenic stress relieving approaches or profiles that are in use today.

These usually involve a heating or warming cycle that is repeated multiple times in sequence.

Every part or component has its own particular challenges, so every item should be considered individually. But, in general, the most beneficial cryogenic treatment is employed when the part is in its rough form and before final cut, polish or grind. This provides that the component is in a stabilized and stress relieved condition when critical tolerance cuts are applied. Such parts will not experience the "creep" or "walk" that is often experienced on non-cryogenically stress-relieved parts. Parts that go out of round or fail to maintain flatness on final machining will benefit from cryogenic stress relief. By using cryogenic stress relieving, manufacturing yields will increase, quality will improve, and tolerances will be held to more exacting specifications.

2.4.12 SHRINK FITTING [III]

Shrink fitting is a method used to insert a pin or bushing into a housing or other assembly requiring an extremely tight tolerance fit. Our shrink fitting process can be used as an alternative to conventional press fitting, or more likely, to permit a mechanical fit that otherwise could not be accomplished via the mechanical force of press fitting.

During the cryogenic shrink fitting process, the insert is cooled via exposure to a cryogen, typically carbon dioxide solid or liquid or liquid nitrogen in order to reduce its size through the contraction usually associated with reduced temperatures. A companion operation of heating the housing or other part that receives the insert is conducted to enlarge the opening by taking advantage of the expansion usually associated with increased temperatures.

While it is not always necessary to use both heating and cooling in combination, the most demanding shrink fitting applications, including those with the tightest tolerances, often require this multi-step approach. Care should be taken when using any cryogen and consideration of the material and relative masses needs to be considered carefully. In addition, because steels may be subject to additional transformation when exposed to cryogenic temperatures, additional processing either before or after may be warranted. Heating of metals for expansion should also be controlled and not induce unnecessary thermal stress on the component during the shrink-fit process.

At the Cryogenic Institute of New England, Inc., they have successfully accomplished numerous shrink fitting projects. These include very large steel pipes, sized at over 24 inches diameter to very intricate miniaturized parts. Some satisfied customers from our diverse client list include large multinational companies, US Department of Defence contractors, research labs, transportation companies, including trucking, air and railroads, to name a few.

2.4.13 MATERIAL SEPARATION [III]

The Cryogenic Institute of New England, Inc. offers material recovery or reclamation by cryogenic material separation techniques. Cryogenic material separation is a process that exploits the different coefficient of thermal expansions of products that are made up of different types of materials. A simple example is copper wire clad in plastic or other insulating wrap. By utilizing cryogenic material separation, the contraction of frozen copper, coupled with the expansion of the bonded compound, can produce a sheer force that promotes separation of the two materials.

This process is carried out in different scenarios that utilize one of our cryogenic chambers or vessels. Precise time and temperature profiles are used to promote maximum separation. In many cases, the objective is to recover an underlying substrate or metal element that has been over-coated and/or bonded to an elastomeric or insulating compound. Cryogenic material separation is ideal for thermoplastics, PVC, nylon, polyethylene, and polypropylene, synthetic and natural rubbers, etc. and all metals.

Some examples of applications include high value precious metals recovery, recovery of steel reinforcements from oil well seals, removal of moulded or bonded materials that have cured and were misapplied or not in specification when applied and waste stream separation.

2.5 CRYOGENIC TREATMENT PROCESSE [7]

A fundamental distinction among different CT is given by the parameters of the cooling-warming cycle. In two families depending on the minimum temperature reached during the cycle are categorized:

• Shallow Cryogenic Treatment (SCT) or Subzero Treatment: the samples are placed in a freezer at 193K and then they are exposed to room temperature.

• Deep Cryogenic Treatment (DCT): the samples are slowly cooled to 77 K, held- down for many hours and gradually warmed to room temperature.

• In some cases, the actual temperature could be higher than the nominal one because of thermal insulation limits, especially after a significant exploitation of the system and the consequent ageing of the chamber seals.

• Each new material needs to be treated and tested at different temperature levels, in order to identify optimum conditions. In most cases, two or three temperature levels are enough to obtain a quick indication in the selection of a specific temperature by means of microstructural changes investigation (i.e. calorimetry or acoustic emission);

• Hold time over 36 hours does not bring significant improvements and in most cases 24 hours are enough to obtain results;

• Cooling rate values range is restricted in order to prevent thermal-shock cracking. Commonly, the applied values vary from 0.3 K/min to 1.2 K/min.

• In many cryogenic systems warming rate is not closely controllable and little importance to this parameter is given in literature despite of some suggested hypobook about carbides precipitation during the warming phase.

2.5.1 CRYOGENIC TREATMENT SYSTEMS

A cryogenic system is equipment which allows controlling temperature in the cryogenic range into a chamber, using liquid nitrogen or helium. Until the end of the Sixties, any attempt to perform CT had been done by direct immersion into liquid nitrogen, with the catastrophic result of cracking the components. The cryogenic treatment system developed by Ed Busch (Cryo- Tech, Detroit, MI) in the late 1960s and later improved by Peter Paulin (300 Below Inc., Decatur, IL) with a temperature feedback control on cooling and heating rate, allows to perform effective a rack less CT. As a result, many companies have developed systems to perform CT, mainly in the USA and in Canada, but also in China, India and Japan.

The three most important cooling systems are described in:

• Heat Exchanger: the liquid nitrogen flows through a heat exchanger and the output cooled gas is diffused inside the chamber by a fan. There is no contact between nitrogen and samples.

• Direct Nebulization: the liquid nitrogen is nebulized directly in the chamber or in a cavity around the chamber. A fan allows to obtain a homogeneous temperature distribution; the liquid nitrogen is dispersed around the samples.

• Gradual Immersion: the samples are immersed into the liquid nitrogen for a specific time, then they are extracted and gradually led back to the room temperature by means of a flow of temperature controlled air.

Another type of cooling system is the so-called "Hybrid System", which combines direct nebulization and gradual immersion during different phases of the cooling process, in order to reduce liquid nitrogen consumption.

2.5.2 DIRECT NEBULIZATION CRYO-SYSTEM.

Reference 2.15 shows the layout of a direct nebulization cryogenic system. The Control Unit (CU) receives the temperature information from the sensor (S) placed in the chamber (C). The CU operates on the electro valve (EV) by the regulation of the liquid nitrogen flow through the injectors (I). The fan (F), which is controlled by an electric engine (E), helps to diffuse the nitrogen homogeneously. The CU allows to control the cycle parameters and it provides a print of time temperature diagram. In a direct nebulization system with a chamber of about 0.25 m3, an ordinary cycle requires from 1000 l to 2000 l of liquid nitrogen usually stored in a tank (T), depending on cycle parameters and on the treating material quantity.

2.5.3 CRYOGENIC TREATMENT CHAMBERS

Cryogenic chambers, or cryo-chambers, come in a variety of sizes and for reference duration. The chambers are typically designed to accommodate batch or continuous loads and come in two styles, frontloading and top loading. Just like equipment, the appropriate design will depend upon the production volume and part con reference duration of a plant. Some examples are shown below.

- **Top-loaded Cryogenic Box Freezer**

The top-loading for reference duration shown in reference offers excellent use of floor space and is an economical solution for small production volumes. By using liquid nitrogen as the cooling medium, the chamber is suitable for shrink fitting, cold treatment and deep cryogenic processing. Technicians can process different part sizes and for reference duration in the same load, in equipment conreferenced to run in batch mode. The chamber is loaded manually or by using a hoist or overhead crane. The interior is made of stainless steel as is all piping and components that are exposed to the liquid or cold nitrogen gas. Some models use painted structural steel for the outer shell.

- **Front-loaded Cryogenic-Cabinet Freezer**

The chamber in reference has a side-hinged door. The height of the chamber can be aligned with automated part transfer equipment such as might be part of a heat treatment processing line. Interior dimensions accommodate a standard heat treatment basket. Workers can also load the chamber with a hand truck.

- **Front-loaded Cabinet Freezer**

The chamber shown in reference can accommodate a very large number of small parts such as saw blades, inserts, or drill bits. The unit uses a programmable control system for controlled cool down, process time and warm-up. The vertical design promotes efficient cooling. Parts are loaded onto trays or shallow baskets and loaded into racks.

- **Cryogenic Tunnel Freezers**

Continuous process equipment like the one in reference can accommodate large production volumes of parts with similar sizes and for reference duration. Easily integrated as part of a production cell, manufacturers of machined consumable items blades, knives, drill bits and end mills rely on this type of equipment to keep up with production requirements for cold treatment. Equipment manufacturers based the design on proven technology from the frozen food industry creating a reliable processor with readily available replacement parts.

- **Cryo Freezer Model** [IV]

- **Product Features**

Stable, long-term preservation of cells and tissues can be achieved by reaching ultralow temperatures. Temperatures generally lower than surrounding -130 degree C, create a state where ice crystals become amorphous. That is the recrystallization point of pure water of the glass transition Temperature of water. Even if cryoprotective agents are used to assist in the preservative function, recrystallization can occur at opproximately-115 degree C. Recrystallzation within and outside the cells may cause damage to the samples, Maintaining an ultralow temperature of -156 degree C, far lower than the recrystallzation point, maintains vitrification of the samples without crystallization.

GENERAL SPECIFICTIONS

- -100 C to-156 C.
- Fast cooling
- Down feed evaporator for most efficient refrigerant flow
- High capacity air-cooled condenser with dual condenser fans, aerodynamically designed fan blades

CUSTOMER BENEFITS

- Safer, more convenient then liquid Nitrogen freezer
- Superior in cost/performance to liquid nitrogen freezer
- Top-to-bottom temperature uniformity dramatically improved
- Lowering operating costs then Liquid Nitrogen freezers of similar capacity
- 100%of storage volume 156 liter is usable
- Washable condenser filter keeps fins free of dust to maintain peak cooling efficiency; no tools required for remove

FEATURES

- CFC-free refrigerant.
- Stable cryogenic temperature of -148 C~-156 C. without Liquid Nitrogen
- Patentes, Cryo refrigeration system are mix refrigerant flow systems.
- I.D.P Control system(integrated data processing system)
- Remote Telecommunication Monitoring and control(R.T.M)alarm system
- Monitoring system
- Chest Cabinet construction
- Access port of 1"(2.54cm) diameter with cap
- Recessed heavy-duty swivel casters
- Automatic timer and restart delay functioning circuit built for protection.

I.D.P CONTROL SYSTEM(INTEGRATED DATA PROCESSING SYSTEM)

- Touchpad data entry system and wide LCD display of all functions
- Set point security system with user password
- Main power and alarm clocks in temperature and alarm set points
- High/low limit alarm functions with factory-set defaults for quick start
- All set points adjustable in 0.1 C increments
- LN2/L. CO2 back-up program
- Data printing system
- Audible/Visual alarm system with setting warning point temperature or relative temperature realm setting

REMOTE TELECOMMUNICATION MONITERING AND CONTROL(R.T.M)ALARM SYSTEM

- power failure or temperature deviation triggers audible and visual warming
- Continuous charge battery back-up system provides full alarm function in case of power failure
- Operation event telephone alarm system
- Digital battery indicator displays battery capacity
- Touchpad alarm test function physically warms internal probe to simulate alarm condition
- RS-232 data port with system software package(option)
- Extreme alarm contacts for connection to remote system.

- MONITORING SYSTEM
- Lifeguard compressor protection monitor performance and automatically adjusts to internal and external conditions, extending compressor life
- The temperature of cabinet, warm/cold, Liquid Nitrogen Back-up are monitoring
- Printer mode Thermal or P.C Printer
- Extreme ambient alert warms if room temperature affect performance
- Voltage indicator advises of low/High Voltage source indications
- Clean filter indicator light advises when to remove and wash condenser filter

CHEST CABINET CONSTRUCTION

- Low profile design for access to inventory

- Heavy-duty counter-balanced lid with personal password lid locking for security

- Double seal lid gaskets to minimize frost build-up
- Independents sub-loads provide additional protection
- Minimum 180mm foamed-in-place urethane insulation, closed cell, CFC-free, to protect product against high ambient conditions
- Heavy-gauge steel cabinet with high-impact powder paint finish
- Rounded interior for easy cleaning
- Access port of 1"(2.54cm)diameter with cap
- Recessed heavy-duty swivel casters

INVENTORY SYSTEM AND ACCESSORIES

- Optional inventory components including racks, boxes and divider may by be ordered separately or as full-load-inventory systems (Back-up system mechanical assembly : option)

- See Accessories section for information on optional free-standing N2 back-up system

- Inventory components, validation test ring(6point), calibration certificates and associated products

- Telephone sound card

APPLICATION

- Cryogenics freezers, Conqueror are designed for long-term storage of biological at uniform temperatures of -156 degree C, safely below the -130 degree C. glass transition temperature of water

- Cell viability is improved because biologically relevant, thermally driven reactions are not known to occur

Performance			Interior	Exterior	Power	AMP
CFQ-156	132L	-156°C	W600 x D400 x H555	1540 x 850 x 1050	220V/3P	12A
CFQ-300	300L	-140°C	W1050 x D470 x H610	2120 x 850 x 1080	220V/3P	12A

- 50/60Hz conqueror available
- PSF-156 available as same size as CFQ or at custom-made spec.

2.5.4 BUOYANCY-DRIVEN CRYOGENIC SYSTEM [10]

The cryogenic apparatus designed for his research, as shown in Reference2.22, included a liquid nitrogen storage bucket, buoyancy mechanism, thermocouple, temperature indicator, temperature recorder, and cylindrical water tank. The diameter and height of the water tank were 150 mm and 1020 mm, respectively. The liquid nitrogen storage bucket was a heat-insulated cylindrical tank with the outer diameter of 350 mm, inner diameter of 220 mm and height of 300 mm. The volume of the liquid nitrogen was about 10 liters. An 80 cm long metal tube with a sealed bottom was placed inside the liquid nitrogen storage bucket as a cryogenic treatment chamber for the specimens. The clearance between the opening of the liquid nitrogen bucket and the metal tube was sealed with heat insulation materials to reduce the evaporation of the liquid nitrogen. Because the temperature of the upper section of the metal tube was high (near room temperature), and the bottom section was low (near -196°C), the specimen to be cryogenically treated was first suspended by a cotton string in the upper section of the metal tube. A flow meter was used to control the flow rate of water into the retort on the right side, which controlled the speed of descent of the specimen in the metal tube. Thus, the temperature decrease rate of the specimen could be controlled. When the specimen dropped to the bottom of the metal tube, the inflow of the control of water was turned off and the water was held in the retort. After a predetermined length of time, the water outflow valve was opened and the outflow rate was regulated to control the speed of ascent of the specimen in the metal tube, as well as to control the temperature rise rate of the specimen. The conditions of cryogenic treatment in this experiment are shown in Table 2.9, with needle valves controlling different water inflow and outflow rates in order to control the temperature fall and rise rates of the specimens. The cryogenic treatment procedures in this experiment were as follows:

(1) The temperature detecting point of the T-type thermocouple 1 was fixed to the specimen, and the specimen was put into the specimen basket.

(2) The recording rate of the temperature recorder was properly set.

(3) The water inflow needle valve modulated and adjusted for a given water inflow, enabling buoyancy to raise the counterbalance weight, and to make the specimen descend slowly.

(4) When the specimen reached the bottom of the metal tube, the needle valve controlling water inflow was closed, and the specimen was held for a predetermined time.

(5) After being held for the required time, the water outflow needle valve was modulated for an appropriate amount of water outflow, enabling the balancing weight to descend, and then allowing the specimen to ascend slowly until it reached room temperature.

- **Temperature Distribution in the Cryogenic Treatment Chamber**

Reference 2.22 shows the apparatus for cryogenic treatment designed in this experiment, which differed from commercial cryogenic equipment in the temperature control of the work pieces. The metal tube with its lower section placed in the liquid nitrogen as the cryogenic treatment chamber of the work piece. When the metal tube was placed in the liquid nitrogen container, the temperature inside the tube dropped gradually, but after a specified period of time, the temperature distribution no longer changed in the regions remain unaltered and stable for the cryogenic treatment periods significantly. Reference 2.23 shows the temperature distribution in the metal tube after it had been in the liquid nitrogen bucket for (a) 2 hr and (b) 4.5 hr. From Reference 2.23, it can be seen that the temperature held at around room temperature in the upper section of the metal tube and dropped gradually along the lower sections until the temperature of liquid nitrogen (-196°C) was reached at the bottom of the tube. The variation of temperature was smooth along the tube. There was no significant difference between the two temperature distribution curves in Reference 2.23, indicating that the temperature in the tube reached a stable state without any significant variations after the metal tube was in the liquid nitrogen bucket for two hours.

- **Temperature Increasing and Decreasing Curves**

To ensure that the temperature of the workpieces could fall and rise slowly and smoothly in the cryogenic treatment process, a buoyancy-driven apparatus was used for cryogenic treatment of the workpieces. A flowmeter with a needle valve was used for to control water inflow and outflow in order to control the temperature decrease and increase rates of the workpieces. The different water inflows controlled by the needle valve of the flowmeter were numbered, as shown in Table 2.9. Different water inflows resulted in different temperature decrease times and thus the average temperature decrease rate could be calculated. When the water inflow rates were adjusted from high to low at 8.6, 7.4, 5.7, 4.0, and 3.1 (cm3/min), the corresponding changes in area are average temperature decrease rates were: 0.57, 0.49, 0.38, 0.27, and 0.20 (°C/min), respectively. As shown in Reference 2.24, the cryogenic treatment curves in the temperature reduction processes were all smooth regardless of the water inflow rate, and the temperature reached that of liquid nitrogen in the end. After the workpieces were kept at the temperature of liquid nitrogen for a predetermined time, the needle valve of the flowmeter was modulated to control the water outflow rate and raise the workpieces. Different water outflows controlled by the needle valve of the flowmeter were numbered, as shown in Table 2.9. Different water outflows resulted in different temperature increase times and, thus, the average temperature increase rate could be calculated. When the water outflow rates were adjusted from high to low at 6.7, 5.7, 5.0, 3.2, and 3.1 (cm3/min), the corresponding temperature increase rates were: 0.45, 0.38, 0.33, 0.21, and 0.20 (°C/min), respectively. As shown in Reference 4, the cryogenic treatment curves in the warming processes were all smooth no matter what the water outflow rate.

- **Comparison of Cryogenic Treatment Curves**

Reference 2.25 shows the entire cryogenic treatment curve with the water controlled at different inflow and outflow rates. As shown in Reference variations of this temperature were very smooth in the temperature decrease stage (AB), temperature maintenance stage (BC), and warming stage (CD). Reference 2.26 shows one of the temperature variation curves of workpieces cryogenically treated using a commercial gas-cooling apparatus. It took 9.5 hr for the temperature of workpieces to decrease to the temperature of liquid nitrogen, and they were maintained at low temperature for 30 hr. Afterwards the supply of liquid nitrogen was stopped to allow the temperature of the workpieces to rise to room temperature naturally. As shown in Reference 2.26, except for the temperature increase stage, which had a smoother variation of temperature, there were drastic fluctuations in temperature, with an average fluctuation margin of about 30°C. This phenomenon was closely related to the cooling principle of the apparatus.

The heat-exchange-cooling apparatus for cryogenic treatment used in industries also controls the temperature of the workpieces by controlling the injected amounts of liquid nitrogen. However, the injection rate of liquid nitrogen can only be corrected when the temperature deviates from the target temperature, thus resulting in fluctuations with large amplitudes in the cryogenic treatment curves. The temperatures of two different positions in the apparatus, one on the workpieces and the other near the workpieces, were recorded with the temperature recorder. These results are shown in Reference 2.27. As seen, the temperature curve of the point on the workpieces was smoother during the temperature maintenance stage, with an abrupt rise in temperature at the beginning of the temperature increase stage. As for the point beside the workpieces, whether during the temperature holding or increase stages, temperature fluctuations occurred. From these temperature curves it was evident that the commercial apparatus for cryogenic treatment used in industries, although a microcomputer was used in temperature control, could not lower the temperatures of the workpieces to that of liquid nitrogen. Abrupt fluctuations in temperature also occurred. In a process such as this, internal stress would be generated due to thermal shock which would reduce the service life of the work pieces.

In general, for a commercial cryogenic apparatus, an injection of liquid nitrogen is used to lower the temperature of the workpieces and the temperature is controlled by adjusting the injected amount and frequency of injection of liquid nitrogen. Because the injection of liquid nitrogen is intermittent, the temperature of the workpieces fluctuates and the abrupt rise or fall in temperature generates thermal stress in the workpieces, which results in serious setbacks in stabilizing the microstructure or in eliminating the internal stress during the cryogenic treatment. The buoyancy-driven apparatus designed in this experiment allowed the workpieces to maintain smooth temperature decrease and increase rates without fluctuations. Also, the capital expense was lower than that of any cryogenic apparatus currently on the market, and the temperature of the workpieces easily reached the temperature of liquid nitrogen (around -196°C), which resulted in more effective cryogenic treatment.

There are many advantages to the buoyancy driven cryogenic apparatus designed in this experiment. Not only did it reduce the capital cost of equipment, but the temperature of the workpieces could be controlled steadily and smoothly without fluctuations. Thus, thermal stress would not occur, and the microstructure of the treated materials should remain stable. Also, the temperature of liquid nitrogen could be reached (-196°C), ensuring the effectiveness of the cryogenic treatment. Moreover, since liquid nitrogen does not require gasification or conveyance through piping, the consumption of liquid nitrogen would be lowered and, therefore, the expense of cryogenic treatment significantly reduced.

2.6 BRAKE INFORMATION [11] [12]

Some interesting terminologies for brake are described here.

2.6.1 BRAKE PERFORMANCE

Brake Performance is level of brake torque produced and the resistance to brake torque loss. For performance do not use the term stopping distance because that involves more than just the brakes. Make it clear there is a difference between making a brake system feel better and actually perform better. The stopping distance of a car is not necessarily directly related to the feel. A poor feeling brake system can have very good performance, i.e. Jaguar. While a great feeling system can have lousy performance, i.e. Ford Focus. Basically, you need a bigger rotors and good pads with the best contact patch possible between the two. Also higher friction levels with higher coefficient of friction brake pads.

2.6.2 BRAKE FADE

Brake fade is the loss of brake torque due to items other than mechanical failure. Basically, fade is caused by over use of the brakes to the point where a majority of the fluid pressure and/or pad friction is lost. This is caused by heat, as heat is created in the brake system it causes the brake fluid to boil and that introduces air into the system. If enough brake fluid is transformed into a gas you will not be able to create the required brake pressure to stop the vehicle. On top of this the same heat causing the fluid to boil is also breaking down the pad and dropping its coefficient of friction. This is commonly referred to as pad fade. To avoid fade is very easy, you can use a fluid with a higher boiling point and/or a pad with a more advantageous temperature vs. coefficient of friction curve. You can also introduce cooling into the system with brake air ducts, vented rotors, rotors with more vent surface area and overall better ventilation in the corner area. Loss of braking efficiency from excessive thermal stress.

There are three separate and distinct types of brake fade:

1. Pad fade: When the temperature at the interface between the pad and the rotor exceeds the thermal capacity of the pad, the pad loses friction capability due largely to out gassing of the binding agents in the pad compound. The brake pedal remains firm and solid but the car won't stop. The first indication is a distinctive and unpleasant smell, which should serve as a warning to back off.

2. Fluid boiling: When the fluid boils in the calipers, gas bubbles are formed. Since gasses are compressible, the brake pedal becomes soft and "mushy" and pedal travel increases. You can probably still stop the car by pumping the pedal but efficient modulation is gone. This is a gradual process with lots of warning.

3. Green fade: When the pad is first placed in service the first few heat cycles will cause the volatile elements of the material to out gas. The process is continuous throughout the service life of the pad, but it is most pronounced in the bedding in process when the out gassed materials form a slippery layer between the pad and the disk reducing the coefficient of friction to near zero. Once the pads are bedded in out gassing is so slow as to not be a problem unless the effective temperature range of the pad is exceeded.

2.6.3 BRAKE FEEL

Brake feel is pedal effort and pedal travel for any given desired deceleration. Ease of brake pressure modulation, accuracy and precision of modulation. Feedback through the pedal "describing" pad rotor contact dynamics and pressure fluctuations. Brake feel is just like steering feel. The better the feel/feedback is the more of the inherent performance you will actually be able to use.

2.6.4 DYNAMIC BRAKE CONTROL

Is a "Panic Assist Feature" what it does is measure the velocity of pedal travel by using either a sensor on the pedal or in the booster. If a certain threshold is met then the booster (if it's an electronic booster) or the DSC pump will apply max pressure. It doesn't actually stop the car in any shorter distance than you could. The reason for DBC if that it's been established than many people when emergency braking will ease off the brake pedal a little after the initial stab. DBC keeps the pressure up even if anyone let off. This can be a real pain when anyone trying to modulate the brakes applying by yourself as most systems have a pretty low threshold and just aggressive braking is seen as a "panic stop." This feature also requires a functioning ABS, the expensive systems are electronic so if the ABS fails the feature is disabled, but some cheaper cars have a purely mechanical system and a failed ABS is not detected. Imagine what happens when you have max brake power and no ABS.

2.6.5 ABS TECHNOLOGY

Anti Lock braking systems sense the speed and rate of deceleration of each of the wheels of a vehicle independently and, through a microprocessor control system, act to prevent lock up of any of the tires under braking force by cycling the line pressure to the wheel that is approaching lock up. Most current passenger cars are fitted with ABS.

2.6.6 COEFFICIENT OF FRICTION

A dimensionless indication of the friction qualities of one material vs. another. A coefficient of 1.0 would be equal to 1g. The higher the coefficient, the greater the friction. Typical passenger car pad coefficients are in the neighborhood of 0.3 to 0.4. Racing pads are in the 0.5 to 0.6 range. With most pads the coefficient is temperature sensitive so claims that do not specify a temperature range should be viewed with some suspicion. The optimum is to select a pad with a virtually constant but decreasing coefficient over the expected operating range of temperatures. As a result, the driver does not have to wait for the pad to heat up before it bites, and the pad fade will not be a factor so that modulation will be easy.

2.6.7 CRACKING

Cracking is primarily due to heat cycling that weakens the cast iron discs. The exact mechanism of this failure is disputed. Cast iron discs are formed with the excess carbon being precipitated in the form of carbon plates or flakes dispersed throughout the ferrite (iron) matrix. What is believed to happen is that when discs are operated above about 900° F, the carbon becomes more flexible or "fluid" in its shape partly in the material due to the thermal expansion of the enclosing ferrite matrix. Then, as the disc cools relatively rapidly back below about 900° F the carbon is trapped in a changed more random shape then when it was first cast. This creates internal stress on the part and continuously transforms the disc by relieving the stress through the cracking. The cracks begin by appearing between carbon flakes. Nodular or ductile iron would resist this cracking due to the excess carbon being precipitated in a spheroid form, but it, like other alternative materials do not have the mechanical properties needed to function ideally in a brake disc application. In discs that are cast to resist cracking through chemistry and controlled cooling at the foundry, cracking will still occur, but more slowly and take the form of heat checks on the surface. In some cases cracks will begin at the periphery of the disc and propagate inwards. In this situation, propagation can be delayed by drilling small holes at the end of the cracks (stop drilling). We do not recommend this however, because if the cracks continue to propagate unnoticed, catastrophic mechanical failure will result. Replace disc at the first sign of cracks at the outer edge of any size. A historic note, the original purpose of the curved or angled vane disc was to prevent cracks from propagating by imposing a solid vane in the path of the crack. The cooling function was secondary.

2.6.8 BRAKE DISC

The rotating portion of a disk brake system. Mechanically attached to the axle, and therefore rotating with the wheel and tire the disc provides the moving friction surface of the system while the pads provide the stationary friction surfaces. Except for racing, discs are normally manufactured from one of several grades of cast iron. Some European front drive passenger cars, where the rear brakes do very little work, are using aluminum metal matrix rear discs to save weight. Most professional racing cars use carbon/carbon discs.

1. One-piece disc: A disc cast in one piece with its hat or bell. This is the inexpensive way to manufacture a disc and is perfectly adequate for normal use. There are some tricks to the design to reduce distortion.
2. Floating disc: The norm in racing, the floating or two-piece disc consists of a friction disc mechanically attached to the hat either through dogs or through drive pins. Properly designed this system allows the disc to dilate (grow radially) without distortion and to float axially, greatly reducing drag.
3. Solid disc: A disk cast as a solid piece suitable for light cars not subjected to extreme braking.
4. Ventilated disk: A disc cast with internal cooling passages. The norm in racing, high performance and heavy vehicles.

2.6.9 FRICTION MECHANISMS

For a pad and disc to function as a brake there has to be the conversion of kinetic energy to heat. There are two primary models of the mechanism of this conversion; both involve the breaking of bonds to release energy. In the case of the abrasion model the bonds broken are the ones already existing in a materials. The bonds are broken due to the chafing or abrasion of a harder material or particle in direct contact with it. The second model is the adhesion-breakage model where temperature and pressure at the interface between the pad and disc surface cause the fusion of one material to the other or the diffusion of one material into the other. In this case, the instantaneous bonds formed in the process are broken releasing energy. Pad materials function using both models at the same time or at different times. The abrasive mechanism predominates at lower temperatures but is also necessary to control build- up of low melting point pad materials at elevated temperatures where the adhesion breakage mechanism is thought to predominate. The adhesion-breakage model requires a transfer layer of pad material to be established on the disc surface to function unless the brake system is designed so that the disc is fusing into the pad. The latter is the case with many high dusting European automotive designs where the disc wears observably as the pad wears. The iron in these discs is typically " "softer" more dampened form of cast iron.

2.6.10 WEAR SENSORS

To ensure that pads are replaced before they are worn down to the backing plates, several types of wear sensors are employed. Most production cars are designed with a float in the master cylinder reservoir. When the pads have worn to the minimum permitted thickness, enough fluid has been displaced to ground the float and complete an electrical circuit that activates a warning light on the dash. Alternatively some cars use an electronic wear sensor in the pad. This type of sensor typically is worn through when wear limits are reached, breaking continuity in the sensor circuit. As such, it needs to be replaced if the light has come on. There is another less expensive method used where the pad has a thin but stiff tab riveted to the pad backing plate that rubs on the disc face and squeals when the wear limit is reached. In some modern racecars used in long distance events, calipers are fitted with more complex electronic sensors and circuitry to warn the drivers and, by telemetry, the crew of the pad condition.

CHAPTER 3
PROBLEM FORMULATION

To find out effect of improvement in wear resistance of brake rotors designed a methodology. Similar types of brake rotors and liners are purchased and given them treatment at -80 deg. C and -193 deg. C. Untreated and treated rotors are used in motorcycle for equal braking. Wear of any part causes material removal which results in loss of weight and change in dimension. So these are sufficient parameters to measure the wear. Rotor 1 was treated for sub zero treatment, Rotor 2 was cryo- treated and Rotor 3 was untreated.

3.1 RESEARCH METHODOLOGY

- Procure brake rotors and its liners of similar size and material.
- Dimensional measurement of brake rotors i.e. inside rotor diameter after marking.
- Weight measurement and Hardness measurement of all rotors and liners.
- Surface roughness measurement of brake rotors.
- Cryogenic treatment at temp. of -80 deg. centi. by mechanical refrigeration and & -193 deg. centi. Deep Cryogenic Treatment.
- Weight measurement of rotors.
- Use of treated and untreated rotors for equal braking cycles.
- Wear measurement of brake rotors and liners by dimensional measurement and weight measurement.
- Testing for various mechanical properties of treated and untreated rotors.

3.2 TREATMENT AT -80^0 C (MECHANICAL CASCADE REFRIGERATION)

Mechanically refrigerated systems normally provide cooling by exchanging heat with the air. In this book work one set of material is treated mechanically at 193.15 K (-80°C) by cascade refrigeration apparatus available at L.D College of engineering.

We all known that cascade refrigerator is working with 2 different boiling point refrigerants, our laboratory equipment operates with R-13 & R-502. The maximum lower temperature reached by laboratory equipment is 188.15 K to 178.15 K (-85°C to -95°C) approx.

Two stage cascade refrigerator which is used for mechanical cooling treatment at 193.15 K is as shown in reference. Cascade refrigeration system capable of this is 208.15 K or better behave similarly to the single stage models and have the same operational consideration.

The second stage of a two stage unit is designed to only start when the first stage has achieved a certain level of heat removal. In addition the second stage has circuitry that prevents the two stages from attempting to start simultaneously, thus reducing the compressor start up surge current. Proper line voltage, air flow to heat exchanger both inside and outside the chamber, and proper ventilation are all essential for proper operation. It is traced that most problems with cascade system to one or three of these three causes. Cascade refrigeration system by nature is more delicate than their single stage counterparts. The basic scheme of cascade operation is to use one compressor that is cooling an intermediate heat exchanger to about zero deg. C. the condenser coil of the second stage compressor is the other half of the intermediate heat exchanger. The evaporator of the second stage removes heat from the chamber work space and transfers it to the intermediate heat exchanger. The second stage compressor is a separate refrigerant circuit that uses special ultra low temperature refrigerant. The first compressor generally has an air cooled condenser coil that exchanges the heat to the room air. Balance of performance between two stages is critical and therefore should only be serviced by a technician who is familiar with this type of system.

Because of the extremely cold evaporation temperatures of this system, atmospheric moisture will accumulate on the evaporator coil even more rapidly than with the convectional refrigeration equipment. In addition to the reduced system capability caused by evaporator coil icing, this condition is more stressful to a cascade system than it would be for a single stage system. The precautions in the single stage refrigeration are, allowing atmospheric moisture to enter the chamber are even more critical when using a chamber with cascade refrigeration. Current version of the programmable controller incorporates automatic refrigeration control. When using non programmable versions of temperature controllers and when the automatic refrigeration control is not used, care should be exercised to avoid unnecessary running the system for long periods at high temperatures with compressor on. Again it is important to periodically make sure that air heat exchangers is clean and not obstructed by lint , debris or anything else.

3.3 TREATMENT AT -196^0 C (LIQUID NITROGEN)

The unique treatment chamber comprises a fully insulated box with a removable or hinged top and a parts platform (uniformly perforated) located a short distance above the inside bottom surface of the chamber. A cryogenic liquid delivery pipe enters the treatment chamber at a point near the top of one of the chamber's side walls and extends downwardly to a point near the bottom of the chamber. The delivery pipe has a liquid discharge port (or extends as a delivery manifold) below the parts platform attached and introduces the cryogenic liquid to the chamber without splashing or splattering such liquid on parts and items supported on the platform, thereby avoiding detrimental thermal shock of such parts and items frequently causing cracks and fractures therein. Temperature measurement and liquid level monitoring sensors provide indication of processing conditions within the treatment chamber for direction of the processing program to optimize treatment results and efficiencies.

The unique methodology of the invention provides for the carrying out of the time-temperature processing cycle profiles related to the total weight of the parts being processed in the ultralow temperature treatment chamber. The process cycles include a sequence of modes of operation including: (a) descend (ambient temperature to -200.degree. F.) over 3-24 hours without part contact with any cryogenic liquid; (b) grid-level (-200.degreeF to -280.degreeF) over 1-12 hours, again with no submersion of parts in the cryogenic liquid; c) pre-soak (-280 degree. F to -300 degree. F) over the 0.5 to 13 hours with submersion of parts in the cryogenic medium of up to 50% to 75% of the maximum liquid level height; (d) soak (-300 degree F to-320.degree F) for 24 hours with submersion of parts in the cryogenic medium of up to 75% to 100% of the maximum liquid level height; and (e) ascend (-320 degree F to ambient) for 8 to 46 hours with the cryogenic liquid allowed to evaporate (boil off) until the chamber is free of such medium and the chamber temperature has reached ambient.

In Reference 3.5 there is presented a series of time-temperature diagrams showing processing mode profiles for the cryogenic treatment of a number of treatment chamber loadings of metallic parts in accordance with the invention. Treatment mode periods are indicated for chamber loadings of 54 kg, 127 kg, 453 kg, 907 kg and 9072 kg of the metallic parts.

Through practice of the methodology of the invention, and utilization of the treatment chamber apparatus thereof, substantial improvement in part wear ability has been achieved with high reliability and repeatability. Thus, for example: high silicon steel alloy drill bits have shown a life improvement of 2 to 1 over untreated bits; carbide faced milling tools have shown a life improvement of 4 to 1; high-nickel hobs (used by turbine blade manufacturers) have shown a life improvement of 3 to1; stainless steel razor blades have shown a life improvement of 15 to 1; and copper electrodes an improvement of 6 to 1.

One or more submersion heaters may be cycled on-off during the ascend mode to assure that a uniform temperature ascend profile is maintained. Liquid levels are adjusted within the descend, grid-level, pre-soak, and soak modes in accordance with multiple temperature sensors.

Referring initially to Reference 3.6 is shown in a perspective view, partially cut away, an ultralow temperature treatment chamber 10 for carrying out deep cryogenic processing of metallic, carbide, ceramic and plastic parts and items to greatly improve their resistivity to abrasion wear, corrosive wear, and erosion wear in accordance with the present invention. The chamber 10 is comprised of front and rear walls 12 and 14, respectively, side walls 16 and 18 and a bottom wall 20. These walls are all formed of a relatively thick center layer of insulating material, such as a rigid foam plastic material, with an inside sheath of aluminum alloy sheeting and outside welded sheath of steel sheeting of adequate thickness to provide structural integrity to the chamber 10 to support and contain the load of materials (parts or items) to be processed within the chamber. The inside metallic sheathing must be sealed at all seams (as by welding) to provide a liquid-tight inner shell for the chamber. The chamber size is dictated by the size and number of parts that the user desires to process in a single treatment batch. The chamber, therefore, may be fabricated to hold as little as 50 pounds of parts and have an effective internal processed-parts volume of 1 cubic foot, or the chamber may be constructed (with appropriate outer sheath structural reinforcement) to hold 20,000 pounds or more of parts and have an internal processed-parts volume of 250 cubic feet or more.

The chamber 10 is provided with a removable top 22 or with a hinged lid. The top 22 or lid is comprised of a relatively thick layer of insulating material and outer steel plate 26. As in the case of the chamber walls, an insulation layer 24 comprises part of top 22. The insulation material is encased in an inside sheath of steel sheeting and such sheath is appropriately welded to top plate 26. Whether hinged to chamber 10 or structured to be entirely removable, the chamber top 22 must be designed to provide sealing closure of chamber 10 during the ultralow temperature processing of parts therein. Thus, an appropriate number of latch-lock fasteners 28 must be provided around the periphery of the top 22 for engagement with mating fastener means 30 affixed to the upper portions of the front, back and side walls of chamber 10.

The lower portion of cryogenic treatment chamber 10 is provided with a removable raised parts support platform or grid 32 (may be supported above bottom wall 20 as by brackets 32a) to provide a space 34 (between bottom wall 20 and platform 32)for the initial charge to the chamber of cryogenic liquid. The platform or grid 32 is thus uniformly perforated with small holes 32b for the passage of the extremely cold vapor (evaporating from cryogenic liquid in space 34) or cryogenic liquid itself into the upper areas of chamber 10 for cooling contact with parts P supported on platform 32 and undergoing ultralow temperature treatment in accordance with the invention. The cryogenic liquid cooling medium (preferably liquid nitrogen having a boiling point temperature of -320.degree. F.) is introduced to the bottom area 34 of chamber 10 through a fluid feed pipe or conduit 36 which extends downwardly from its upper chamber entry pipe section 36a to its fluid discharge end 36b. As shown in Reference

3, the feed pipe 36 may be connected at its lower end 36b to (and feed) a fluid distribution manifold 36c which includes side rows of uniformly spaced perforations or ports 36d. The feed pipe 36 is fed with cryogenic liquid through supply line 38 extending through chamber wall 16. The rate of liquid feed through line 38 is controlled and directed by a pulse rated solenoid valve 40 as described hereinafter. The manifold or phase separator 36c sits in a slightly elevated position (as by support legs, not shown) above bottom wall 20 and such position and the arrangement of manifold or phase separator perforations or distribution ports 36d results in a substantially uniform distribution and mixing of the cryogenic liquid over and throughout bottom area 34 of the chamber 10. Thereby, particularly for large size treatment chambers, the evaporation of the cryogenic liquid to cooling vapor is highly controllable and uniform over the liquid surface and upwardly into the upper areas of the chamber 10. The feed pipe discharge end 36b (Reference 3.7) or co reference uration of the manifold 36c (when utilized as shown in Reference 3.8) and the perforated platform 32 design (supporting the parts and items undergoing ultralow temperature processing) cooperate to prevent splattering and splashing of cryogenic liquid onto the materials on the platform thereby avoiding the occurrence of sudden damaging thermal shock to such materials. Splashing and splattering of cryogenic liquid within chamber 10 is also avoided by the controlled relatively slow entry rate of such liquid into the chamber through the manifold's distribution ports 36d until the mixing pool of cryogenic liquid in the bottom of the chamber has reached a pre-programmed level.

At the top of the treatment chamber 10, positioned appropriately on the front, back and/or side walls, there is located one or more gas exhaust vents 42, with associated exhaust piping 44, so that warmer gas or vapor (accumulating near the top of the chamber) can escape the chamber carrying out the heat energy given up by the materials under treatment within the chamber. Also mounted at the bottom of one or more of such walls (or on the chamber floor 20) are submersible strip heater units 46 which (as described hereinafter) are utilized during the part of the processing cycle wherein temperature ascent is affected. For further use in connection with the control of the temperature ascent portion of the processing cycle, there is provided one or more gas circulation fans 48 which depend from inside the chamber top or lid 22 and/or are mounted at the top of the chamber walls and are driven by appropriate fan motors 50 controlled by the time-temperature program circuitry.

Along the height of side wall 18 there are positioned quench control sensors S-1, S-2, S-3, S-4 and S-5 which monitor the level of the cryogenic liquid in the treatment chamber and report the varying liquid levels to t"e system's process cycle control center. Sensor S-1 is located about midway between bottom wall 20 and platform or grid 32 and sensor S-2 is located at the grid level. Sensor S-5 is located at the point of maximum permissible liquid level within chamber 10 and below the entry height of feed pipe 36 (height of entry pipe section 36a). Sensors S-3 and S-4 are positioned intermediate sensors S-2 and S-5 with appropriate spacing. Positioned on the side wall 16 of chamber 10 are electronic temperature sensors T-1, T-2, T-3, T-4and T-5 located at the same levels within the chamber as the liquid level sensors S-1 to S-5 to measure the temperature of the ultra cold vapor circulating about the parts under treatment in the upper part of the chamber and of the cryogenic liquid in the lower part of the chamber. The treatment chamber 10 may be provided with a second set of temperature sensors T-1 to T-5 located on one of the other walls of the chamber at like vertical locations with the temperature sensed by each pair of sensors T-1,T-2, etc. being averaged by the process control circuitry so that more accurate measurement of the temperature conditions within the chamber is obtained for utilization in control of the cryogenic treatment program.

Reference 3.7, as a front section view of the treatment chamber of Reference 3.6, should be referred to for its showing of the elevation relationships of the parts support platform 32, quench control sensors S-1 to S-5 and temperature sensors T-1 to T-5. Such reference also shows the positions of the gas exhaust vents 42 and heaters 46 on the chamber walls at the bottom of the chamber 10, as-well-as the position of the circulating fans as shown as 48. Reference 3.8, as a top section view of the treatment chamber of Reference 3.6, referred to for its showing of the for reference duration of the cryogenic liquid distribution manifold or phase separator 36 (when it is used in large treatment chambers) and the position of the rows of liquid discharge ports 36 to assure substantially uniform fluid distribution and mixing of the cryogenic liquid entering chamber 10 below the parts support platform or grid 32.

Referring now to Reference 3.9, there is shown in schematic block diagram fashion the principal components and operational systems, with interconnection, of the ultralow temperature treatment system of the invention. The cryogenic treatment chamber 10is shown to contain parts platform 32, liquid distribution feed pipe 36, exhaust gas vents 42, heaters 46 and circulation fans 48, as-well-as liquid level sensors S-1 to S-5 and temperature sensors T-1 to T-5. A process program controller 52 is interconnected to the treatment chamber so as to receive liquid level measurements from sensors S-1 to S-5 (via transmission cable 54) and temperature measurements from sensors T-1 to T-5 by transmission cable 56. Information relative to the weight of the parts to be treated within chamber 10 is input to the controller 52 (load weight settings 58) along with appropriate time-temperature cycle data (cycle profile settings 60). Control of the cryogenic treatment process, to and through the "soak" mode, is accomplished by controller 52 (including its software program) through direction (via cable 62) of pulse rated solenoid valve 40 (located in cryogenic liquid supply line 38), thereby initiating and regulating the rate of flow of cryogenic liquid to the fluid distribution feed pipe 36. Supply line 38 connects to cryogenic liquid supply vessel 64. Following the 24 hour "soak" mode the temperature "ascend" mode is commenced with the termination of all cryogenic liquid feed into chamber 10 and, in accordance with the "ascend" mode temperature rise profile (set into the software program followed by program controller 52), the controller initiates the operation of heaters 46 and circulation fans 48 (as required) via direction communicated through cables 66 and 68, respectively. The heaters and circulation fans are utilized, as required, to speed up the evaporation of the cryogenic liquid within the treatment chamber and maintain the pre-programmed temperature profile during the "ascend" mode and return the chamber and its parts contents to ambient temperature.

3.4 LIQUID NITROGEN USAGE [IV]

Liquid nitrogen is what most cryogenic processing companies use to cool the parts in their machines. Here are some facts about liquid nitrogen that may be useful.

1. The use of liquid nitrogen does not pollute the air. The atmosphere is about 78% nitrogen anyway. Liquid nitrogen is produced by cooling air down until it liquefies. So using liquid nitrogen just puts the nitrogen back where it came from.

2. No, you cannot recycle and use the liquid nitrogen over. The way nitrogen cools a part is by absorbing the heat from the part and becoming a gas.

3. The boiling point of LN2 is -320.4°F at 1 atm. (195.8°C, 77.4°K, and 139.3°R)

4. The heat of vaporization is 38.8 K Cal/Liter or 579 BTU/Gallon

5. 1 Liter of LN2 makes 22.8 ft^3 of gas at Standard Temperature and Pressure (STP)

6. LN2 weighs 6.745 pounds/gallon

7. LN2 should be used in a ventilated area. Too much used in a closed area will dilute the oxygen in the room and can cause asphyxiation.

8. Never touch LN2, it is extremely cold and can cause extreme frostbite.

9. Get training on the use of LN2 and always wear protective gear when using it.

10. Nitrogen was discovered by Daniel Rutherford in 1772

11. Nitrogen has a specific heat of 2.04 kj/kg K°

12. Nitrogen is the fifth most abundant element in the universe

13. Nitrogen freezes at -345.9°F. (-209.9C or 63.2°K)

Liquid Nitrogen is the chief cost of cryogenic processing. The more you use, the more it costs, So let's take a look at how much it is necessary to use. Note that the only reasonable way to compare our machines with our competition"s machines is to compare like cycles with the same weight of parts in the machine. One excellent way of comparing machines is to know how much nitrogen it takes to run the machine through a particular cycle with nothing in the machine. That is why we give you the following information.

- Cooling the Load

First, you need to cool the parts that you are treating. The most commonly treated material is steel and cast iron. It takes a quarter of a liter of LN2 to cool one pound of steel or cast iron down to -300°F. So for every 45 kg of steel you need to process, you need 25 liters of LN2 just to cool the parts.

- Cooling the Machine

The inside of the machine also has to be cooled to -300°F. The interior of cryoprocessors are generally made of steel. So if you have a machine that has an interior made of 90 kg of steel, you need 50 liters of liquid nitrogen to cool that interior.

- Machine Insulation Efficiency

Heat always makes its way past the insulation and into the machine from the outside atmosphere. There are many paths for heat to take. The overall efficiency of machine's insulation can be expressed as the number of liters of liquid nitrogen it takes to maintain the machine at 88.7K. We publish these numbers along with the weight of the internal structure so that you can calculate the amount of nitrogen it will take to run any particular load.

- Nitrogen Usage For Applied Cryogenic Machines

	CP-200vi	CP-500vi	CP-1200vi
Interior Weight	54 kg	90.7 kg	181.4 kg
Nitrogen Usage to maintain the machine at -300°F	5 Liters/Hour	7 Liters/Hour	11 Liters/hour
Zero Load Nitrogen Use	150 Liters	218 Liters	364 Liters

The cycle for to calculated the nitrogen usage for each of our standard machines.

- Cryo Processing Cycle Used

Ramp Down	8 Hours
Hold	20 Hours

The calculation of the Nitrogen usage is done as follows:

1. First calculate the nitrogen used to cool the interior of the machine or "dead weight" as it is sometimes called. To do this multiply the interior weight in pounds x by volume 0.56 liters/kg.For a Cp-200vi, this is 54 kg times 0.0.56 liters/kg=30 liters

2. Next, calculate the nitrogen used to make up for insulation losses during the ramp down part of the cycle. The rate of heat flow into the machine is directly proportional to the difference between the temperature outside of the machine and inside the machine. This means is the overall heat flow into the machine during the ramp down is one half the total heat flows into the machine for the same period of time when the machine is down at -300°F.

So in the case of a CP-200vi and an 8 hour ramp down, the nitrogen used is .5(5 liters/hour x 8 hours) = 20 liters

3. Calculate the amount of nitrogen used to maintain 88.7K for the 20 hour hold part of the cycle.

For the Cp-200vi, this is 5 liters/hour X 20 hours = 100 liters

You can see that it will take about 150 liters to run this program in an empty CP- 200vi. If you add the nitrogen needed to cool the load, you can tell how much LN2 will be needed for any particular load.

Different metals need different amounts of LN2 to cool them to 88.7K. For purposes of estimating LN2 usage, the following values will get you fairly close.

- Requirement of Nitrogen to cool 0.45 kg of Metal

Steel	0.25 L
Aluminum	0.58 L
Copper	0.23 L
Tungsten	0.08 L
Magnesium	0.325-0.625L

Table 3.1 Nitrogen usage for diff. Processors

Standard Cryogenic Processors by Applied Cryogenics, Inc.			
	CP-200*vi*	CP-500*vi*	CP-1200*vi*
Inside Diameter	22 inches	31 inches	40 inches
Chamber Depth	33 inches	46 inches	63 inches
Chamber Volume	7 cubic feet	17 cubic feet	42 cubic feet
Electrical	220v 1 phase	220v 1 phase	220v 1 phase
Amps	20	20	50
Program Capacity	8	8	8
Machine "dead weight"	120 Pounds	200 pounds	400 pounds
Liquid Nitrogen use at -300°F	5 Liters/hour	7 Liters/hour	11 Liters/hour
Zero Load Nitrogen use	150 Liters	218 Liters	364 Liters
Max Tempering Temperature	+320°F	+320°F	+320°F
Microprocessor Control	Yes	Yes	Yes
Chart Recorder	Yes	Yes	Yes
Price as of 3/29/11	$36,500	$47,500	$64,000

CHAPTER 4
RESULT AND ANALYSIS

4.1 MEASUREMENT BEFORE USE

TABLE 4.1 DIMENSIONAL MEASUREMENT OF BRAKE ROTOR
(INSIDE DIAMETER OF BRAKE ROTOR)

LOCATION	ROTOR-1	ROTOR-2	ROTOR-3
1-7	110.16mm	110.10mm	110.12mm
2-8	110.18mm	110.10mm	110.15mm
3-9	110.15mm	110.11mm	110.17mm
4-10	110.16mm	110.12mm	110.13mm
5-11	110.15mm	110.12mm	110.15mm
6-12	110.16mm	110.10mm	110.15mm

TABLE 4.2 WEIGHT MEASUREMENTS OF ROTORS

ROTOR-1	1248.0gm
ROTOR-2	1244.5gm
ROTOR-3	1232.5gm

TABLE 4.3 HARDNESS MEASUREMENTS OF ROTORS

ROTOR-1	216 BHN
ROTOR-2	227 BHN
ROTOR-3	216 BHN

TABLE 4.4 DIMENSIONAL MEASUREMENTS OF LINERS

LOC	LINER 1		LINER 2		LINER 3	
	A	B	A	B	A	B
1	7.00	7.10	7.31	7.25	6.95	7.38
2	6.89	7.12	7.31	7.15	6.96	7.37
3	6.81	7.21	7.38	7.10	6.90	7.45

(All Dimensions are in millimeter)

TABLE 4.5 WEIGHT MEASUREMENTS OF LINERS

LINER NO.	A	B
LINER-1	94.5gm	92.5gm
LINER-2	94.5gm	94.0gm
LINER-3	93.5gm	93.0gm

TABLE 4.6 SURFACE ROUGHNESS Ra OF BRAKE ROTORS

	ROTOR UNTREATED	ROTOT -80 °C TREATMENT	ROTOR -185 °C CRYO.TREAT.
Ra VALUE BEFORE USE	4.80	4.20	4.94

TABLE 4.7 EFFECT OF TRETMENT ON HARDNESS

	ROTOR -80 °C MECH.TREAT.	ROTOR -185 °C CRYO.TREAT.
BEFORE TREATMENT	216 BHN	223 BHN
AFTER TREATMENT	223 BHN	227 BHN

4.2 MEASUREMENT AFTER USE

TABLE 4.8 WEIGHT MEASUREMENTS OF ROTORS

ROTOR WITHOUT TREATMENT	1229.5gm
ROTOR -80 MECH. TREATMENT	1242.5gm
ROTOR -185 CRYO.TREATMENT	1243.5gm

TABLE 4.9 WEIGHT MEASUREMENTS OF LINERS

LINER NO.	A	B
LINER-1	94.5gm	92.0gm
LINER-2	94.5gm	94.0gm
LINER-3	93.0gm	92.0gm

TABLE 4.10 SURFACE ROUGHNESS Ra OF BRAKE ROTORS

	ROTOR UNTREATED	ROTOT -80 °C TREATMENT	ROTOR -185 °C CRYO.TREAT.
Ra VALUE AFTER USE	2.40	1.99	3.07

TABLE 4.11 WEIGHT ANALYSIS AFTER 2000 BRAKING FOR BRAKE ROTORS

	ROTOR WITHOUT TREATMENT	ROTOR - 80 °C TREATMENT	ROTOR -185°C TREATMENT
INITIAL WEIGHT (A)	1232.5gm	1245.0gm	1244.5gm
WEIGHT AFTER 2000 BRAKING (B)	1229.5gm	1242.5gm	1243.5gm
WEIGHT LOSS FOR USE (A-B)	3.0gm	2.5gm	1.0gm
PERCENTAGE INCREASE			
FOR EXAMPLE LIFE IN YEARS	03 YEARS	4.8 YEARS	09 YEARS

TABLE 4.11 WEIGHT ANALYSIS AFTER 2000 BRAKING FOR LINER

	A	B	TOTAL
INITIAL Wt. OF LINER W/O TREATMENT	93.5gm	93.0gm	186.5gm
WEIGHT AFTER USE	93.0gm	92.0gm	185.0gm
WEIGHT LOSS FOR USE			**1.5gm**
INITIAL Wt. OF LINER -80 °C MECH.TREAT.	94.5gm	92.5gm	187.0gm
WEIGHT AFTER USE	94.5gm	92.0gm	186.5gm
WEIGHT LOSS AFTER USE			**0.5gm**
INITIAL Wt. OF LINER -185 °C CRYO.TREAT.	94.5gm	94.0gm	188.5gm
WEIGHT AFTER USE	94.5gm	94.0gm	188.5gm
WEIGHT LOSS AFTER USE			**0.0gm**

TABLE 4.12 SURFACE ROUGHNESS Ra COMPARISION OF BRAKE ROTORS

	ROTOR UNTREATED	ROTOT -80 °C TREATMENT	ROTOR -185 °C CRYO.TREAT.
Ra VALUE BEFORE USE	4.80	4.20	4.94
Ra VALUE AFTER USE	2.40	1.99	3.07
CHANGE IN Ra VALUE	2.40	2.21	1.87

CHAPTER 5
CONCLUSION

Cryogenic Processing is not a substitute for heat-treating. Cryogenic Processing is not a coating. It affects the entire volume of the material. It works synergistically with coatings. These benefits extend to cast iron, aluminum, stainless steels, and other materials.

From the result and analysis it is clearly observed that the wear resistance of brake rotors and liners are improved dramatically. Cryogenic Treatment at -195°C is more effective than Mechanical Refrigeration (Cascade) at -80 ^{O}C. Cryogenic treatment improves the wear resistance of brake rotors by three times by comparing the weight reduction after 2000 braking cycle . As the braking cycle increases after use the effort for braking increase.

The surface roughness Ra value is well retained after use which is measure for better braking response due to increase in friction. Untreated rotor contact surface becomes more smoother than treated rotor surface.

Following advantages are experienced by cryogenic treatment

- Stronger
- Safer
- 300% increase in wear resistance
- Stops brake warping
- Brake pads seat better
- Stops micro cracking
- Improved stopping distance
- Better "tracking" when under near "lock-up" conditions especially when in conjunction with today"s advanced, computer assisted Anti-Lock Braking Systems.

CHAPTER 6
SCOPE OF FUTURE WORK

- ## Multistage Cryogenic Treatment

The multistage cryogenic treatment is a more advanced process that has been developed as an evolution from the conventional ones. In this treatment, the isothermal soak at cryogenic temperature is substituted by several cryogenic cooling /heating phases. This process is more effective but its main advantages is that it is much faster, an average of fifteen hours for the whole process than the conventional ones.

- ## Cryogenic Helium Processing

The cryogenic Institute of New England, Inc. introduces a new capability of utilizing liquid helium for cryogenic treatment of materials to temperatures as low as 4K. Measurements were recorded by attaching a spring loaded silicon diode cryogenic temperature sensor rated to 1.4K with a calibrated accuracy of +/- 10mK. The chamber utilizes multiple dedicated delivery systems for introduction of both liquid nitrogen and liquid helium.

- ## Experiment for disk type brake rotor

In this research work experiment was performed on the brake drum and expanding liner type brake. Instead disk type brake rotor can be utilized and same type of treatment and wear analysis can be performed for both two wheelers as well as four wheelers.

- ## Sub zero treatment at -80°C with Cryogen

In this experiment sub zero treatment was given by Mechanical Cascade Refrigeration System for comparison with cryogenic treatment. This sub zero treatment can be also given by a liquid cryogen. Cascade refrigeration utilizes indirect heat exchange and liquid cryogen can cool by direct cooling.

CHAPTER 7
REFERENCES

PAPERS

1. Robin Alan Rhodes, "Cryogenic Treatment For Motor Sports", Cryogenic Institute of New England, Inc., Worcester, Massachusetts 2008.
2. John Bellah, "Cryogenic Brake Rotors", Police Fleet Manager Magazine, November 2005.
3. A. Molinari, M.Pellizari, S.Gialanella, G.Streffelini and K.H.Stiasny, "Effect of deep cryogenic treatment on properties of tool steel", in proceedings of conference on Advance Materials Processes Technologies,1999,pp.1461-1469.
4. Daniel H. Herring "Cold and Cryogenic Treatments", dherring@heat-treat-doctor.com, May 2005.
5. Frederick Diekma, "Cold Facts About Cryogenic Processing" Controlled Thermal Processing Inc., Antioch, Ill. & Rozalia Papp, Air Liquide U.S. LPCountryside, Ill., October, 2009.
6. Richard N. Wurzbach, "Improving Component Wear Performance Through Cryogenic Treatment", OMA-1, CLS1, William DeFelice2 Maintenance Reliability Group, Brogue, Pennsylvania.
7. P. Baldissera and C. Delprete, "Deep Cryogenic Treatment: A Bibliographic Review", Politecnico di Torino - Dipartimento di Meccanica, Corso Duca degli Abruzzi 24, 10129 Torino, Italy , The Open Mechanical Engineering Journal, 2008.
8. Robin Alan Rhodes, "Cryogenic Treatment For Motor Sports", Cryogenic Institute of New England, Inc., Worcester, Massachusetts 2008.
9. Keith Howerd, "Icing The Cake, Most engineers think of heat treatment as a hot process. Deep Cryogenic Tempering will force them to think again".
10. Yong-Chwang Chen and Han-Ming Chen, " A Cryogenic Treatment Apparatus With Steadily Descending Rate of Temperature", Journal of the Chinese Institute of Engineers, 2010, Vol. 33, No. 6, pp. 909-914.
11. Michael Romano, Mechanical Engineer, "Vehicle Brake Information", Brake Engineer working at Continental-Teves (trademark: Ate Brakes) and Ford.

12. Stephen Ruiz, Engineering Manager & Carroll Smith, "Glossary of Braking Terminology" Consulting Engineer at STOPTECH LLC.

13. P Sekhar Babu, P Rajrndran, Dr K N Rao, "Cryogenic Treatment of M1, EN19 and H13 Tool Steel to Improve Wear Reasistance", October, 2004.

WEB SITES

I. www.cryoplus.com
II. www.nwcryo.com
III. www.nitrofreez.com
IV. www.metal-wear.com
V. www.heikimanracing.com

BOOKS

A. Chen Jer Ming, M.E. Book "Cryotreatment of Music Wire", National University of Singapore, 2004.

B. Ritesh J. Mistry, M.E. Book "Cryogenic Treatments & Experimental Analysis of its Effects on Tools and Materials", Gujarat University, 2010.

PATENTS

a. Kenneth J. Workman and Dennis W. Pitts, "Method of Treating Brake Pads", U S Patent 5 447 035, 1995.

b. Kenneth J. Workman, "Method of Treating Spark Plug", U S Patent 5263886, 1993.

APPENDIX - A

ABBREVIATIONS

ABC	Anti-Lock Braking System
AISI	American Iron and Steel Institute
CT	Cryogenic Treatment
DBC	Dynamic Brake Control
DCT	Deep Cryogenic Treatment
HSS	High Speed Steel
IIT	Indian Institute of Technology
PC	Polycarbonate
PU	Polyurethane
PEI	Polyethyleneimine
PTFE	Polytetrafluoroethylene
SCT	Shallow Cryogenic Treatment
UHMWPE	Ultra-High-Molecular-Weight Polyethylene

www.ingramcontent.com/pod-product-compliance
Lightning Source LLC
LaVergne TN
LVHW070943160826
845679LV00022B/1893

* 9 7 9 8 8 9 7 2 4 8 3 2 2 *